A CREATIVE STEP-BY-STEP GUIDE

CONSERVATORY
AND GREENHOUSE GARDENING

A CREATIVE STEP-BY-STEP GUIDE

CONSERVATORY
AND GREENHOUSE GARDENING

Author
Sue Phillips

Photographer
Neil Sutherland

AURA BOOKS

5117
This edition published in 1999 by Aura Books
© 1999 Quadrillion Publishing Limited, Godalming,
Surrey, GU7 1XW, UK
Printed and bound in Italy
ISBN 1-90168-391-5

Credits
Edited, designed and typeset: Ideas into Print
Photographs: Neil Sutherland
For Quadrillion: Jane Alexander

The publishers would like to thank Robinsons Greenhouses
of Millbrook, Southampton, UK, for supplying
a greenhouse for photographic purposes.

THE AUTHOR

Sue Phillips is a popular TV and radio gardener, and writes
regularly for a wide range of newspapers and magazines.
A keen gardener since the age of four, she is a qualified
horticulturalist who trained at Hadlow College in Kent. She
has since run her own nursery and been Gardening Advisor
for a leading garden products company. Sue has been a full-
time gardening writer for 15 years and has written over 20
books and contributed to many more.

THE PHOTOGRAPHER

Neil Sutherland has more than 30 years experience in a
wide range of photographic fields, including still-life,
portraiture, reportage, natural history, cookery, landscape
and travel. His work has been published in countless books
and magazines throughout the world.

*Half-title page: A superb collection of cyclamen, calceolaria
and cineraria shown off to full advantage on tiered staging.*

*Title page: In a conservatory or greenhouse you can garden
in comfort and enjoy growing a wide range of plants from
ferns and flowering houseplants to exotic palms.*

*Copyright page: The vivid bracts of poinsettia (Euphorbia
pulcherrima) echo the flashes of colour created by the fish
as they swim near the surface of an indoor pool.*

CONTENTS

THE MANY REWARDS OF GARDENING UNDER GLASS

Gardening under glass gives you all the creative potential of outdoor gardening, but using tender plants. The protection of a glass 'room' makes it practical to grow everything from frost-sensitive species right through to delicate tropical exotics, including those categorised as 'conservatory plants'. (This is a nurseryman's term for many unusual trees, shrubs and evergreens that are too tender to grow in the garden, too big to fit on windowsills and which in any case need more light than they would get inside the house.) A conservatory can be used in a huge range of decorative ways, from 'indoor-outdoor' room settings through Mediterranean patios to complete tropical gardens. A greenhouse, enclosed porch or lean-to plant room can be used as a free-standing plant room, or decoratively as a display area – or, more often, as a combination of the two. But gardening under glass is also gardening made easy. It is perfect for the person who likes results without heavy or regular work. Because you have complete control over the environment, you can avoid many of the pitfalls of outdoor gardening. The covering of glass keeps plants safe from weed seeds and birds, wind and late frosts. The major pests of the garden, such as slugs and snails, are much less trouble under glass, and even traditional problems, such as greenfly, can be tackled effectively but naturally, since the enclosed space makes it practical to introduce beneficial insects to do the job for you. For many people, the biggest benefit of gardening under glass is that it leaves you free to enjoy the creative aspects of growing plants, and simultaneously provides a comfortable and attractive environment in which to enjoy them all year.

Left: Pelargoniums dominate a conservatory display. *Right:* Velvety gloxinia flowers.

Design options

Established conservatories and decorative greenhouses gradually acquire a distinct personality over several years, with the addition of plants, furniture and furnishings. But if you know at the outset what you are aiming for, you can stock and furnish a conservatory in a predetermined style, using ideas gleaned from magazines or by visiting other peoples conservatories. The basic choice is between 'theming' the conservatory as a plant room or a living room. If growing exotic plants is the priority, choose water-resistant furnishings and floor coverings. Here, providing maximum space for plants in the form of attractive but practical staging, shelving, raised beds or large containers is the main form of decoration. Useful plant-friendly accessories include an interior tap or water tank, cane shading blinds, extra ventilators and trellis on walls to house climbers, or fittings in the roof to take trailing plants. Select outdoor-quality garden furniture, such as teak or cast aluminium, which looks good and withstands the humid environment. Avoid rattan, curtains and soft cushions, which will fade and go mouldy.

Where a conservatory is to be used mainly as extra living space, keep to a few large plants that will make an impact without taking up too much room. Check that they are non-poisonous and unlikely to attract a big pest problem. Water-resistant flooring is still the best option, but since the room will be used more like an indoor room and probably heated for year-round use, washable kitchen-style floorings combine looks with practicality. Decorative blinds, plus a few plants mean that the atmosphere inside the room stays more like an indoor room, avoiding strong light, high humidity or extremes of temperature, so that soft furnishings can be left permanently in place, and pine or rattan furniture and any ornaments can be used without risk of deterioration.

Above: This lean-to plant room gets much of its character from a display of working utensils; vintage gardening equipment is becoming collectable nowadays, and teams well with wooden shelves and worktops.

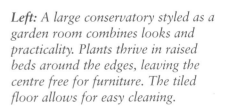

Left: A large conservatory styled as a garden room combines looks and practicality. Plants thrive in raised beds around the edges, leaving the centre free for furniture. The tiled floor allows for easy cleaning.

Right: *If you do not want an 'antique-style' conservatory, then modern ones are also available. Some manufacturers will produce designs to fit awkward sites.*

Below: *A well-planted, attractive conservatory makes a pleasant place to sit and eat or entertain friends. Metal furniture and a washable floor are practical and attractive options.*

A few large foliage specimens, such as this kentia palm, are a good investment.

Above: *In a conservatory designed predominantly for living space rather than for plants, choose a few unfussy plants of the right colour, size and style for their surroundings.*

Flooring options

Where there are plants, there will be spillages. Flooring should be practical, easily cleaned, and not damaged by contact with water or soil. In a greenhouse, price is often the main consideration, but in a conservatory looks matter most; choose an attractive finish that complements furniture and fittings.

Right: Here, the garden seat is handy for enjoying a plant collection and also sets off the plants. White walls reflect maximum light, a useful tip for a room that does not receive much direct sun.

Reconstituted stone paving is easy to clean and provides a firm level surface to support staging. It can be loose-laid over soil.

Ceramic floor tiles have all the advantages of paving but are better looking. Ideal for smarter plant rooms; bed them in cement.

Above: The many practical features in this fine conservatory include ceramic floor tiles; opening ventilators and a solid roof for summer comfort and central heating for winter warmth.

Below: A light, airy, Victorian-style conservatory uses plants for living decoration. In a sunny spot, interior blinds would help to reduce glare and prevent soaring summer temperatures.

Gravel is cheap and easy to remove or replace, but difficult to keep clean. The legs of staging sink in unless stood on tiles.

Quarry tiles are ideal for plant rooms and smart greenhouses. Bed in cement. Treat with red stain or polish.

Right: *This unusual structure is part conservatory and part summer house, combining the main benefits of both. In summer, some plants can go out on the paving, leaving room for afternoon tea inside.*

High-quality vinyl patterns include a very realistic 'natural' wood effect; practical and easy to clean.

The latest linoleum, available in a wide range of colours and patterns, gives a smart, hardwearing floor.

Vinyl flooring can also simulate stone and mineral effects.

Below: *An enthusiast's conservatory packed with plants. Shelving and staging are used to vary the levels. This way, plants are not too congested and are seen to their best advantage.*

Plastic composite floorings are the most rigid, and patterns duplicate a range of hard surfaces, including the wood, marble, and cork shown here.

Left: Fit each roof ventilator with an automatic opener. This helps prevent the greenhouse overheating on sunny days and saves you the inconvenience of having to open and close vents by hand.

Essential equipment

The right equipment helps to make any greenhouse or conservatory quicker and easier to look after. The most basic essentials are staging or shelves to accommodate small plants in pots, and automatic ventilator openers that push the windows open on sunny days to control the temperature. A heater is also essential if you intend growing frost-tender plants through the winter. However, when conservatories or lean-to greenhouses are built against the wall of the house, especially where there are connecting doors, the structure traps much of the heat escaping from the house and this is often enough to keep it frost-free without extra heating. Electric fan heaters are the most commonly used; choose special greenhouse heaters, as they tolerate more damp than the normal domestic kind and are equipped with a built-in thermostat that can be set to maintain the required temperature in winter. Many can also be set to cold and used as air circulator fans in summer. If extra temperature control is needed in summer, install blinds either inside or outside the glass, and put an air circulator fan in the roof. A tap in or near the structure is a useful feature, since watering is the job that will need doing most often. For greater convenience, you could install a hose reel alongside the tap so that the hosepipe can be left connected but coiled away after use. Watering can also be done automatically by growing specimen plants in large self-watering containers, and by fitting staging or pots with a drip-watering system. This can be connected to a timing device on the tap, which switches the supply on and off at preset times. It is also very useful to be able to monitor the growing conditions; a humidity meter and thermometer are handy, and a maximum/ minimum thermometer 'stores' the extremes so you can tell if your heating and ventilation systems are cutting in correctly.

Above: Louvred ventilators can be fitted low into the end or side walls of the house. They increase ventilation by allowing cool air to flow in as hot air goes out through the roof vents.

Above: Louvred ventilators are usually opened by hand on warm summer mornings and closed at night, although special automatic openers can be fitted to this type, too.

Above: In autumn, replace shading with bubble wrap to eliminate draughts and reduce heating costs. Open vents on fine days, otherwise condensation forms inside.

Left: Apply proper shading paint or dilute white emulsion to the outside of the greenhouse in early summer. Wash it off in autumn to give plants light in winter.

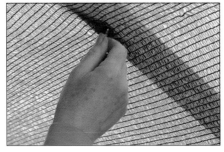

Left: Shading cools the house and protects plants from scorching sun. Fix shading fabric inside the roof and on the sunniest wall, using special clips that fit into glazing bars.

Left: Electric fan heaters are the best way of heating a greenhouse during the winter. Choose a model where the fan can be left running cold in summer to provide extra ventilation.

Above: Use a humidity meter to check growing conditions. In summer, plants enjoy above 70% humidity; in winter, keep it as low as possible, as damp, cold air encourages fungal disease.

Thermometers

A max/min thermometer lets you read the current temperature and monitor the highest and lowest temperature since the device was last set. Reset it morning or night every day. Use it to check that heating is adequate at night in winter, and ventilation in summer.

Below: Digital versions of maximum/minimum thermometers convert to Celsius/Fahrenheit readings at the slide of a switch.

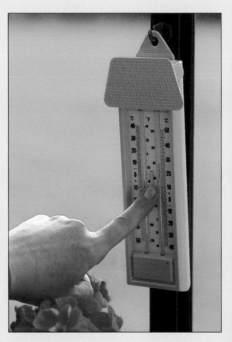

Above: In traditional max/min thermometers, a U-shaped column of mercury pushes a metal splinter to show the lowest and highest readings; both ends of the mercury should read the same, giving the current temperature. To reset, press a central button.

Adjusting a dial-type max/min thermometer

A modern dial-type maximum/minimum thermometer (left) has three hands. The black hand shows the current temperature, the blue one shows the minimum and the red hand the maximum. To reset the thermometer, follow the steps below. Once set, any changes will be obvious next time you check the instrument.

1 First, turn the control knob to the right. This makes the stop on the dial push the blue hand. Move it so it lies directly under the black hand.

2 Rotate the knob to the left so the stop pushes the red hand under the black one. All three hands now show the current temperature.

Feeding and watering

The secret of successful feeding and watering is to match the rate of both to the plant's growth rate. You cannot simply give plants the same amount of feed and water every week all year round; the rates should vary throughout the year, since plants themselves grow faster or slower and so have different requirements. In winter, some plants, such as fuchsias and gloxinias, are dormant and need virtually no water. However, other plants, such as pelargoniums, bougainvillea and cacti, keep their leaves, but need a definite winter rest, with a low temperature, just enough water to prevent them shrivelling up and no feed at all. Most plants need lighter watering and feeding in winter, as they are not growing as quickly as usual. Even tropical evergreens kept at room temperature need a little less than usual, as light levels are lower and they are growing more slowly.

In spring, light levels and warmth increase naturally, so plants start to grow faster and need watering and feeding more often. By the time they have made quite a bit of new growth and are growing quickly, the rate needs increasing again. And in summer, particularly when they are in flower or fruit, plants need most feed and water. As flowers finish and the fruit is picked, decrease the amount of food and water gradually, and continue doing so for all plants as summer comes to an end and outdoor temperatures and light levels fall. Never stop watering suddenly; always cut down gradually, even with plants that become totally dormant.

Right: A liquid feed allows you to vary the rate at which plants are fed, and to change the feed during the season, from a general-purpose one for growth to a high-potash one to promote flowering.

Left: If you forget regular liquid feeding, use slow-release feed tablets instead. Push these down into the potting mixture. They do not dissolve, so replace them every few months.

Below: Two-tier staging with capillary matting on the top tier. Plants that need shade and extra humidity are growing on expanded clay granules below. Watering can be done quickly, using a slow-running hosepipe to damp the tray contents once a day.

Using expanded clay granules in trays

1 *Expanded clay granules are sold specially for use in sub-irrigation benches. They are porous and soak up large amounts of water. Spread out a layer, about 1.25cm(0.5in) deep, over the watering trays.*

2 *Stand pots of plants firmly onto the bed, and keep the granules damp by regular watering according to conditions. The mixture in the pots must be damp to start with or plants will not be able to take up water.*

Using a capillary matting water system

Capillary matting is a fluffy-textured synthetic fabric capable of absorbing many times its own weight of water. Plants standing on it water themselves by drawing up as much moisture as they need by capillary action. For this to work, the potting mixture in the pots must be moist in the first place, so be sure to water plants well before starting up a capillary watering system. Make sure the matting is smooth and use plastic pots with no crocks in the bottom to ensure that the mixture inside the pots is in perfect contact with the matting. When you first lay new capillary matting, it is bone dry and needs to be thoroughly dampened. Spread it out and pour water all over it. From then on, you need only water the front of the matting, as water will move within the material. Capillary systems work best with plants in similar pot sizes with similar mixes and similar watering regimes. At the end of the growing season, roll up the capillary matting as the plants will not need to be kept routinely damp during the winter months. You can reuse the matting for the following season, but first wash and rinse it in garden disinfectant. You will probably need to replace it every two years.

1 Cut the matting to fit inside the watering trays, with the fluffy side facing upwards and the firm underside in contact with the tray. Smooth and press into the corners.

2 To water plants quickly, simply wet the capillary matting. Use enough water to damp the matting well. Any surplus will drain away through gaps in the watering trays.

Above: The easiest way to keep a few larger conservatory plants watered is by using a simple self-watering system. This type uses a bag that feeds a short run of drip line. Each pot has its own nozzle, which adjusts to alter the watering rate.

Right: The bag holds enough water to last several days, even in summer. Top it up as necessary. Liquid feed can be added to the bag; the black colour prevents algae growing inside.

Below: Plants that are short of feed look pale; to replace missing nutrients quickly, spray plants with weak foliar feed. Liquid seaweed extract can be used this way to supply trace elements.

Left: A potting bench gets most use in spring; it should be at a convenient height for working, with everything you need, such as pots and potting mixes, close at hand. Later in the season the bench can be used as normal staging.

Routine tasks

The secret of growing plants successfully is to keep up with routine chores. They need not take long; some people enjoy doing 'little and often', while others prefer to allocate a particular time for their tasks. Watering, feeding and looking out for pests and diseases are required more or less all year round. Other jobs are more seasonal. At the start of the growing season, divide any plants that need it, and repot or topdress others. This is also the time to pot up last year's rooted cuttings or pot on young plants propagated at the end of the previous year. Soon after, they will need 'stopping' to encourage bushiness. As the season progresses, tie climbing plants to supports or train them around climbing frames. At the end of the season, give the greenhouse or conservatory a thorough clean. Take all the plants outside, except those that are too big or heavy to move. Clean the glass inside and out, and wash off any remaining painted-on shading to allow as much winter light as possible to reach your plants. Take up capillary matting from the staging, wash and dry it and store it in clean bags in a shed for the following year. Throw away any that is no longer usable. Wash down the staging and flooring; use a fumigant smoke, candle or wash to kill pest and disease organisms if it is practical to do so. When the fumes have cleared, replace the plants.

Repotting potbound plants

1 A plant needs repotting when its roots form a tight ball inside the old pot. You often see roots growing out through the drainage holes in the bottom. Knock it out of the old pot.

2 Sit the plant in the centre of a pot one size bigger, so the top of the rootball is about 1.25cm(0.5in) below the rim. Fill the gap round the edge of the rootball with fresh potting mix.

3 Firm down the new mix gently; this makes sure that it goes right down to the bottom of the new pot without leaving air pockets that roots cannot occupy, and which will cause the mix to dry out quickly.

Stopping plants

Nipping out the very tips of shoots encourages bushiness. Usually, newly potted cuttings of plants such as fuchsias and pelargoniums need stopping a second time, when the sideshoots resulting from the first 'stop' are about 5cm(2in) long. Use the same technique to 'finger prune' older – or indeed any – plants whenever you spot a long shoot that spoils the shape or when forming the head of standards.

Deadheading and tidying up

1 *Check greenhouse plants regularly and remove dead flower heads as soon as the blooms go over. This prevents a lot of fungal disease. Pick flowers off complete with their stems.*

2 *Dead leaves are another potential source of fungal disease; remove them regularly. They often occur naturally at the base of plants and do not indicate that there is a problem.*

Tying in climbing plants as they grow

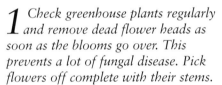

1 *Secure stems to a frame with plant ties or wire clips. Clips reopen easily, so you can add extra stems as you work. This is a passion flower, ideal for a conservatory.*

2 *As the plant grows, fix new stems into place until the frame is thickly covered with foliage. As the pot fills up with roots (around midsummer), the plant will begin to flower.*

Good hygiene

At the end of the season, give a conservatory or greenhouse a thorough clean so there is nothing to cause pest or disease problems during the winter. It is also usually the most convenient time. Start by emptying the structure completely.

1 *Brush out channels in glazing bars, where red spider mite and other pests often hibernate, ready to start an epidemic as soon as the weather warms up in spring.*

2 *Remove capillary matting. In winter, plants need not be kept moist and humid. They need to dry out between waterings then, so occasional hand-watering is best.*

3 *Wash watering trays well, rinse with clean water with added garden disinfectant, and leave to dry. Clean up plants and wipe pots before returning them to the tray.*

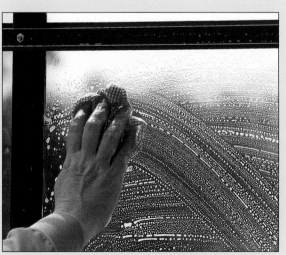

4 *Wash the glass inside and out. Use a sponge and warm water with a few drops of liquid detergent to remove paint-on greenhouse shading and any algae and dirt. In winter, light levels are low and plants need all they can get.*

Staging and displaying

Display techniques are a good way of making the most of under-cover growing space, since the same basic collection of plants can be rearranged regularly or teamed with new pot covers or 'props' to make different displays throughout the season. As well as being easier to look after, a collection of many small pots looks best when raised up on staging. Various types of decorative conservatory staging are available from specialist suppliers; greenhouse firms provide functional solid metal or slatted wooden staging that is easy to clean. Tiered staging allows the most plants to be housed in the least space. Choose shade-loving plants for the lower tiers of greenhouse staging. In a conservatory, choose staging that gets progressively narrower towards the top, so that all the plants receive enough light. Alternatively make your own banked display from planks resting on brick tiers, or simply use flat staging and raise up individual plants by standing them on upturned flowerpots. (Watch the watering, though, as these plants will dry out faster then those on the staging.) Plant very small or 'theme' plants, such as cacti, together in bowls with appropriate 'set decoration' such as driftwood or pebbles. Large striking plants are best potted up to make specimens; stand them on their own in a decorative pot against a suitable background. Some types are suitable for training as standards, which not only take up less room but often look more ornamental. A large collection of conservatory shrubs look good when grouped together attractively and planted in a soil border as a feature. Display climbers by training them over topiary frames, round large hoops, up obelisks or moss-filled wire netting pillars, or over a wall on rustic trellis.

Below: Here, pretty Edwardian-style wire staging is artistically teamed with historically accurate plants for an authentic old-fashioned display. Space the plants out well so that they are not overcrowded.

Left: Simple white-painted wooden slatted staging makes an evocative background for a collection of annual seed-raised green-house pot plants – cineraria, calceolaria and cyclamen – in old clay pots.

Below: *You do not need many plants or props to make an eyecatching display. Choose a few perfect plants and accessories that go well together, then give them enough room so you can see everything properly.*

Streptocarpus flowers all summer and early autumn.

Nephrolepis exaltata 'Bostoniensis' (Boston fern) is a very popular evergreen fern with an arching shape, ideal for displaying on a plinth.

Displaying plants in the greenhouse

1 Upright plants with naturally dangling flowers, such as this fuchsia, lend themselves to being 'lifted', so that they stand out amongst shorter plants.

2 To disguise the upturned pot, stand another plant in front of it. Use tiered staging, shelving and hanging baskets to create a varied display on several levels.

Above: *Create a tiered display in a greenhouse with a narrow shelf above the staging; use this to grow naturally cascading plants, such as trailing tuberous begonias.*

Right: *Use the main staging for bushy, upright plants or climbers trained round wire hoops, with trailing plants along the front. This saves space and looks decorative.*

Greenfly

Right: Greenfly are a common pest under glass. They can be controlled with a natural predator, aphidoletes.

Below: Tip aphidoletes larvae onto damp paper and cover them with a small pot close to affected plants. The adults find the plants when they emerge, and start a good colony.

Affected greenfly turn into brown 'shells'.

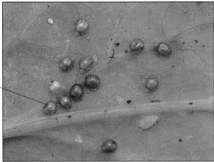

Left: Greenfly parasitized by the gall midge aphidoletes. The mummified bodies hatch out into the next generation of gall midges to keep up the good work.

Red spider mite

Below: Red spider mites are almost impossible to see without a lens. Look out for the telltale damage they inflict: dustlike speckles on foliage, which may turn brown and fall early.

Above: The mites are resistant to most chemicals. Control it with a predatory mite called Phytoseiulus persimilis, *supplied in pots. Open the pots and hang them amongst affected leaves.*

Pest control

Under glass, good growing conditions not only favour plant growth, they also provide the ideal environment for pests and diseases. Insect pests such as greenfly can breed all year round in these protected surroundings, and if fungal diseases appear, their spores multiply rapidly in the warm humid air. Even regular spraying is not a guaranteed solution, since plants are often grown so close together that the leaves are not evenly covered, leaving some organisms untouched. In addition, some pests need specific pesticides to control them, and nowadays it is not unusual to find that some pests also develop resistance to certain products. The best way to keep pests and diseases at bay is to examine your plants regularly. The most convenient time to do this is when watering them; always tackle problems as soon as they appear. Pick off mildewed leaves or blooms, and remove dead flower heads and damaged leaves before they can act as a source of infection. And make use of other non-chemical controls, such as yellow sticky traps. You can trap whitefly by hanging pots of nicotiana above other plants; whitefly particularly like nicotiana and will move onto them, at which point you drop the 'traps' into a plastic bag, dispose of them and put up new ones. A more long-term solution is to use biological control; 'farmed' beneficial insects are available by mail order to tackle a range of common pests. Encourage wild beneficial insects, such as hoverflies and lacewings, into your greenhouse or conservatory by not using chemicals and ensuring that ventilators are left open in suitable weather. Spiders, black beetles and centipedes are also beneficial.

Mealy bug

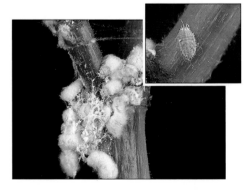

Above: Mealy bug is difficult to eradicate with chemicals as it is usually protected under a waterproof layer of waxy wool. Remove small infestations using the tips of matchsticks wrapped in cottonwool.

Vine weevil

Vine weevils are the fat, white C-shaped grubs that eat entire root systems of cyclamen, primulas and other greenhouse plants. First symptoms are yellowing leaves and wilting. There is no effective chemical control; biological control using a special kind of microscopic nematode worm is the best solution.

1 Nematodes come as a freeze-dried 'powder'. Mix it with water as directed. Mid-spring and late summer/early autumn are the best times to tackle vine weevil larvae.

2 Stir the liquid into a watering can with a coarse rose and spray a steady film of nematode 'soup' over border soil and gravel beds. Also water 'at risk' plants in pots.

Scale insects

Scale insects look like tiny limpets, clinging to the stems and undersides of tough evergreen leaves. Common on lemons, orchids and bay. Their hard covering protects them from many chemical sprays.

Apply a systemic insecticide. After a week, remove dead insects with a cotton bud.

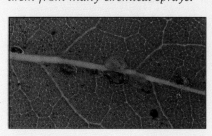

Traps and sprays

Sticky traps are a good non-chemical control for flying insects early in the year, but by midsummer they will also trap the beneficial insects that appear then, so take them down.

Below: *Spray with fungicide to control fungal diseases under glass. Do not apply chemical sprays if you use biological control insects. Follow directions; do not spray in bright sun or onto open flowers.*

Above: *Hang sticky traps above plants to catch flying pests such as whitefly. They are attracted by the colour of these yellow traps and then held fast. Use them just above the tops of plants; disturb the foliage to make whitefly swarm up.*

Whitefly

Above: *Whitefly resemble tiny white moths that congregate on the backs of young leaves and only fly if the plants are disturbed. The young whitefly are 'scales' stuck tight under the leaves, which rarely respond to chemical sprays, so biological control is the best way of dealing with them.*

Below: *The biological control against whitefly is a tiny parasitic wasp, Encarsia formosa. It is supplied as eggs on cards, which you hang onto the affected plants. The wasp larvae feed on the developing whitefly scales which then turn black.*

A hot, sunny conservatory

Most conservatory plants enjoy plenty of sun and reasonable warmth (up to about 29°C/84°F) in summer, but a south-facing conservatory can easily become so hot midseason that a real problem develops and all but a few plants are literally 'cooked'. Shading, extra ventilation and a circulator fan will all help to keep temperatures down. Another solution is to use the conservatory mainly in winter to house plants that need protection from cold, but to stand the plants out on the patio for the hottest part of summer. Citrus plants, conservatory trees and some shrubs are very successful grown this way and make a good outdoor display in a sheltered sunny spot. But for interior conservatory decoration when conditions are very hot and the air is dry, it is vital to choose heat-proof plants. These not only survive 'inhospitable' conditions, but often flower better because of them. Zonal pelargoniums, cacti and succulents are amongst the most tolerant. *Agapanthus africanus* will flower prolifically given a hot summer; it also needs to be slightly potbound to produce a good display of its giant blue or white flower heads. Grow these with blue hesper palm *(Brahea armata)* to make an eye-catching group; the palm has surprisingly soft, architectural blue foliage that makes a good foil for flowers. If you can damp down the floor to keep the air reasonably humid, then *Hedychium* (ginger lily) thrives and flowers best in the heat. Several species are available, all with tall, strap-shaped foliage and huge, wildly exotic spikes of flower. Bird-of-paradise, *Strelitzia reginae*, is another that seems to appreciate heat with some humidity. Plenty of heat and sun encourages it to start flowering within a couple of years. In a humid atmosphere, banana plants make striking specimens and look superb growing in huge terracotta pots. If the plants grow too big, cut them down almost to the rim in early spring and new suckers quickly appear.

Right: The bird-of-paradise plant, Strelitzia reginae, does not usually flower until it is five years old or more, but given heat and sun it then produces successional spikes of large exotic blooms in winter and spring.

Watering plants

Despite being heat-tolerant, all these plants will need frequent watering during hot spells to prevent their leaves turning brown at the tips. Growing them in large containers helps them to stand up to the heat, as the greater volume of potting mixture retains more water.

Oleander
(Caution: poisonous)

Bougainvillea

Scented-leaved
Pelargonium 'Jessel's Unique'

Left: *Agaves are succulent plants naturally adapted to hot, dry, sunny conditions. Although they tolerate a certain amount of neglect, they need care to keep them looking perfect. This is Agave utahensis.*

Blinds and fans

To prevent plants from overheating in summer, use fans and blinds as an alternative to painting the glass of a conservatory with shading paint (which is more appropriate for a functional greenhouse). Aim to keep the temperature below 30°C(86°F). Above this, plants cannot grow well and begin to suffer, even if adequately watered. There is a huge range of decorative conservatory fans and blinds to choose from. They are available by mail order from catalogues or direct from the manufacturers.

Above: *Interior blinds and fans add to the tropical atmosphere, as well as improving conditions so that a much wider range of plants can be grown.*

Musa (banana plant)

Right: *This very luxuriant, tropical-looking display shows just what is possible if the natural tendency of a sunny conservatory to overheat is curbed by the use of fans and shading. The conservatory shrub Tibouchina urvilleana and the orange tree, which are normally very bushy, have been trained as standards to keep them tidy and save space. The oleander is flowering well as it, too, enjoys warmth.*

Left: *Banana plants grow naturally where there is strong sunlight and a high temperature, but they also need high humidity, so damp down the floor daily in sunny weather, and use blinds to protect plants from scorching on the hottest days.*

A shady conservatory

A shady conservatory can house a wide range of fascinating plants. If it is heated to room temperature, virtually all houseplants are candidates. African violets and tropical foliage plants (such as maranta), gardenia, indoor ferns, orchids and bromeliads will thrive. If the structure is only kept frost-free, there are still several possibilities. 'Designer' ivies have extraordinary leaf markings, shapes and textures. Soleirolia – plain green, gold and silver-variegated – is very adaptable and useful for many novel creative schemes. Another good plant for this situation is *Oxalis triangularis*, which has pink flowers and large purple and mauve 'clover' leaves. (Although it dislikes direct sun, the leaves fold up if it is kept too dark.) Tree ferns, such as *Dicksonia antarctica*, make dramatic shapes that suggest primeval forests. Team them with other striking leafy plants, such as *Fatsia japonica, Sasa palmata* (a large-leaved, shade-loving bamboo) and *Trachycarpus fortunei* (a nearly hardy palm) to create a jungly foliage garden. For smaller 'filler' foliage, use near-hardy asparagus ferns, spider plant and tolmiea. Add zantedeschia for dramatic flowers and foliage that are hardy and in keeping with the theme, or decorate with seasonal potplants chosen to suit the temperature at different times of year. Florist's cyclamen, indoor azaleas and forced spring bulbs will all do much better in a cool, shady conservatory in winter than indoors, where it is often too hot and dry.

Above: Dicksonia antarctica *enjoys light, cool shade and lime-free potting mix. Keep frost-free in winter. It can stand outside in summer out of strong sun; hose down the trunk occasionally.*

Right: Indoor azalea, now renamed rhododendron, likes cool shady conditions while in flower. Stand plants outdoors in shade for the summer. Repot soon after flowering only when badly potbound. Use an ericaceous mix and a pot only one size larger.

Repotting aspidistra

1 Crowded stems, a crust on top of the potting mixture and light-coloured leaves indicate a plant that has been in the same pot for a long time, in need of a change.

4 Fill in the space around the roots with new potting mixture. Firm it in lightly and water the aspidistra, allowing the surplus moisture to drain away.

5 Cut off any damaged or yellow leaves. Snip them cleanly away at soil level, leaving no stumpy stems. If repotted in spring, the plant will soon grow new leaves.

2 Even slow-growing plants, such as aspidistra, will need complete repotting every three years. Tip the plant out and gently remove as much of the old mix as you can.

3 Choose a slightly bigger pot and lift the plant into the middle. Sit it on a bed of fresh potting mix at the same level as it grew before.

You can often refresh a plant that is not too potbound by scraping away 2.5cm(1in) of the old potting mix and topping up the pot with a few scoops of fresh mix. Add a little slow-release feed into the new mix.

6 Wipe the leaves with cotton-wool soaked in plain water or use a leaf shine product. These products are only for use on plants with naturally glossy leaves.

7 Stand the plant out of direct sunlight and avoid overwatering. Large aspidistras in good condition are quite scarce and are often passed on from one generation to the next.

Above: *This rattan hamper makes a striking container for a simple collection of soleirolias in silver, gold and plain green, arranged in a chessboard pattern.*

Left: *The ferny foliage of Asparagus meyeri teams well with terracotta, and this is a particularly novel way of growing it. The plants are nearly hardy, so a frost-free conservatory is fine.*

Ferns for shade

Ferns are some of the most versatile plants for a shady conservatory. Their foliage shows off exotic blooms and creates a lush, tropical jungle effect. They can create a cool, tranquil mood with other foliage plants, especially when combined with an indoor pool or fountain. The plants look good grouped with natural materials, though their plain foliage means they also look good with brightly coloured ceramics, reflective surfaces, such as brass or copper, and in front of mirrors. Most ferns look best when allowed to grow into large specimen plants. Repot them annually in spring, into a pot one size larger each time until they reach their ultimate size; from then on topdress them instead. In spring, divide large plants or those that have outgrown their space or are starting to die out in the centre, saving the best pieces to pot back into smaller pots. Feed ferns regularly from mid-spring to late summer with a well diluted, general-purpose liquid feed.

A display of ferns

1 *Choose several gnarled pieces of log; those with a natural covering of lichen or moss look most attractive. Arrange them on the floor as a group in a shady conservatory.*

2 *Place the largest and most striking plant first and give it prime position. This* Blechnum gibbum *makes a distinctive shuttlecock shape.*

Ferns in a basket

1 *Place bark chippings into a lined, shallow wicker basket. (Clean the chippings first by immersing them in boiling water in a bowl and allowing them to cool.)*

2 *Arrange a collection of different ferns in small pots, raising the pots up on the chippings to bring the rims level with the edge of the basket. Use trailing kinds to soften the sides.*

3 *Keep adding more ferns until the basket is completely filled. Choose plants with contrasting foliage sizes, shapes and textures and put them next to each other for a varied effect.*

4 *To complete the display, tuck a few handfuls of previously cleaned chippings between the plants to hide the pots. Kept damp, they also help to create humidity around the plants.*

5 Choose a very small, densely leafed fern to fill a gap at the front of the display, masking the point where the blunt ends of two logs meet. This helps the arrangement to blend into the room and creates a natural look.

3 Position another architecturally shaped specimen next. This unusual climbing fern (Lygodium japonicum), has been allowed to clamber over a short, moss-covered pole.

4 Balance the shape of the display by adding another fern of similar shape to the first, but slightly smaller and with a denser texture. Tuck it into a gap between two logs.

As a general rule, keep indoor ferns at room temperature during the winter. However, they will usually survive at 7-10°C(45-50°F) if kept slightly drier than usual (but not bone dry).

Lygodium japonicum (Japanese climbing fern)

6 The finished display has a good range of shapes and textures, and can easily be altered just by lifting out individual plants and substituting them for others whenever you want.

Blechnum gibbum

5 The finished basket looks good in any shady corner – even on the floor under a table. Since ferns suffer quickly if they dry out, check daily to see if they need watering.

Maidenhair fern

Annual pot plants

Annual flowering plants, such as solenostemon (coleus), primula, exacum and calceolaria, can all add temporary seasonal colour to a permanent collection of conservatory plants. Or, if your conservatory is unheated in winter, use annual flowering plants to decorate it throughout the summer. It is worth growing a few of your favourites from seed, particularly the more unusual plants or new varieties that are not available in nurseries. Good examples include eustoma (lisianthus), *Michauxia tchihatchewii* and torenia. As well as compact plants for shelves or staging, many delicate half-hardy climbers, such as morning glory and rhodochiton, and trailers, such as big, showy double petunias, are all good for growing under cover, especially if you live in a cold region or have an exposed situation

where they do not do well in the open garden. And for winter colour and perfume, tall varieties of stocks, sown in midsummer, make superb plants for a cold, frost-free or heated house.

Below: Cineraria flowers in spring and summer; divide a packet of seed into five or more batches and sow a few every two to three weeks in early and midsummer. Pot plants up as they become big enough to handle. For the biggest and best results, pot the plants on to 13cm (5in) pots later.

Growing solenostemon (coleus) from seed

1 *Wash out a small seed tray and fill it loosely with seed mix from a fresh bag. (Solenostemon seeds are very sensitive.) Level and firm it down lightly with a presser that fits the tray.*

2 *Tip the seeds into your hand and, taking a pinch at a time, sprinkle them thinly all over the surface of the mix. To make it easier, you could mix the seed with dry sand before sowing.*

3 *Cover the seed with a thin layer of vermiculite (no more than one granule deep). It prevents drying out, but because of its colour, it will not prevent light reaching the seeds.*

4 *By sowing thinly, you can leave the seedlings to develop into small plantlets, then pot them up. This cuts out the pricking out stage, when very tiny seedlings are difficult to handle.*

5 *Pot up the strongest and healthiest seedlings, with a mixture of leaf colours and patterns. Pot into 9cm(3.5in) pots filled with good-quality potting mixture.*

Right: *A bank of solenostemon (coleus), pelargoniums and petunias makes a colourful display for a sunny spot. All the plants need a similar regime of feeding and watering, so they can all be treated the same.*

Above: *Persian violet (Exacum affine) makes a naturally neat dome-shaped plant that is covered in perfumed flowers for months. Sow in early spring, and keep the plants evenly moist. They only need small pots.*

Above: *Sow primrose seeds in early spring, leaving the seed on the surface of the potting mixture as they need light to germinate. Keep the seed trays evenly cool, shady and moist.*

6 Solenostemon is native to Java, and enjoys a warm, humid atmosphere under glass. Keep plants out of strong direct sun, water often and nip out the flower buds that develop in the tips of mature plants. This keeps the leaves in good condition for a longer time.

Above: *The feathery flowers of **celosia** are available in many bright **colours**. Sow seed in early spring **in warmth**, and pot into 10cm(4in) pots. Plants flower **from midsummer** onwards.*

Winter pot plants

Winter colour is no problem for the owner of a heated conservatory, since there are plenty of good plants to choose from if you can maintain a temperature of about 10°C (50°F). Several winter-flowering indoor plants, such as cyclamen, cineraria, calceolaria, forced hyacinths and 'Paper White' narcissi, actually do better in a conservatory or greenhouse since they find the central heating indoors far too warm for them and 'go over' fast. For larger containers, there are several shrubby conservatory plants that flower in winter. These include florist's mimosa *(Acacia dealbata)* and the dramatic-looking Ovens wattle *(A. pravissima)*. This has dark green triangular leaves and perfumed yellow flowers in early spring. Train these out flat over a wall or grow as them as small potted trees. *Sparrmannia africana* (house lime) makes a potentially large tree, with huge, hairy, architectural leaves and clusters of lime-like flowers, unfortunately not scented; keep it compact by growing it in a pot. A degree of root restriction also encourages it to flower more profusely. Correa is a family of attractive, bushy Australian shrubs, with plenty of reddish, white or coral pink, bell-shaped winter flowers, depending on variety. If trellis space is available on the walls, you could add winter-flowering *Solandra hartwegii* (huge, yellow, perfumed flowers), *Lapageria rosea* (waxy, pink, bell-shaped flowers), or *Jasminum polyanthum* (sprays of strongly scented white flowers). Otherwise, grow them in large pots and train the stems round support frameworks to make them into free-standing specimens.

Right: Old clay pots of Cyclamen coum and Iris 'Katherine Hodgkin' make a colourful display early in spring, ideal for staging in an unheated greenhouse or conservatory.

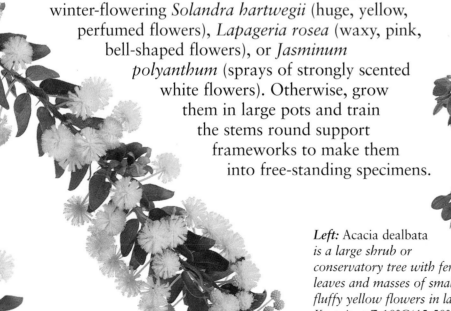

Left: Acacia dealbata is a large shrub or conservatory tree with ferny leaves and masses of small, scented, fluffy yellow flowers in late winter. Keep it at 7-10°C(45-50°F) in winter, and if possible, stand it on the patio in summer.

Left: Rhododendron simsii (Azalea indica). Plants flower from late autumn until early spring. Keep cool, shady and moist, and deadhead regularly.

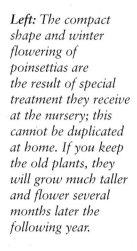

Left: The compact shape and winter flowering of poinsettias are the result of special treatment they receive at the nursery; this cannot be duplicated at home. If you keep the old plants, they will grow much taller and flower several months later the following year.

Left: The winter cherry is a popular plant, usually treated as an annual. The white flowers are followed by berries that ripen through buff-yellow to orange and finally red. The decorative fruits are not edible.

Right: Turn a corner of a conservatory into a real indoor garden by bedding a mixture of seasonal potplants, such as these Primula x kewensis and hyacinths, with permanent shrubs.

Left: Indoor azaleas thrive at 7-10°C(45-50°C) while in bloom. Grow them in a cool conservatory and move plants to a frost-free greenhouse after the flowers are finished. Repot into a barely larger pot in spring, using ericaceous mixture, and stand plants outside in a cool shady place for the summer, protected from pests.

35

Ornamentals for an unheated house

In a greenhouse or conservatory without any form of heating the best plan is to grow plants that naturally flower early outdoors, such as camellia and Christmas rose *(Helleborus niger)*. Grow them in large pots outdoors in summer and move them under glass in late autumn. The protection of cold glass will encourage these plants to flower many weeks earlier than usual, and since they are safe from bad weather you will be able to enjoy perfect blooms in comfort. Ordinary, unprepared spring bulbs, especially dwarf kinds that naturally flower early, also make good, colourful, temporary pot plants. Choose *Narcissus cyclamineus, Cyclamen coum*, named snowdrops, such as the large-flowered 'Magnet', *Iris danfordiae, I. reticulata* and *Eranthis hyemalis*, plus early-flowering alpines, such as saxifrages. With small plants such as these, group a number of pots together in large containers and hide the pots under a layer of moss to make a mini landscape. Alternatively, bank them up with rockery stone or in raised beds edged with dry stone walling to make them into attractive displays. Move pots under cover in late autumn to advance bud development so that they flower earlier than outdoor plants, and replace them in the garden after flowering is over. Winter-flowering pot plants and spring bedding in tubs create masses of colour. And use plenty of foliage plants to create extra interest amongst the flowering displays. Keep plants on the dry side during winter (but not dust-dry), and feed flowering plants occasionally with very weak liquid tomato feed.

Right: *The variegated form of* Fatsia japonica, *plus spring flowering* Kalanchoe blossfeldiana *and* Chlorophytum comosum *make an attractive tub for an unheated house.*

Foliage plants

Aspidistra
Aucuba
Bonsai plants
Cordyline palm
Cryptomeria and other
   colourful conifers
Fatsia japonica
Hebe (variegated)
Ivies (including variegated kinds,
'tree' forms, frilly leaved ones)
Red-, pink- and cream-striped
   Phormium
Trachycarpus

Plunging pots of alpines in a sand tray

1 Display ever-green and spring-flowering alpines by plunging their pots to the rim in moist lime-free sand (not builder's sand). This insulates roots and keeps them moist without rotting.

2 As well as providing ideal growing conditions for these attractive plants, the sand sets them off by making each one stand out individually. Water the sand just enough to keep it just moist.

Below: *Many early spring flowering plants that are perfectly hardy are seen at their best if they are moved into an unheated greenhouse in late autumn. This way, their flowers open earlier than usual and are protected from damage caused by severe weather. You can also enjoy them in comfort yourself.*

Right: *An alpine house is a specialist type of greenhouse for delicate rock plants that dislike winter wet; it has no heating but unusually good ventilation. It can also be used, as here, for displays of seasonal plants, brought in from adjacent cold frames when approaching their best and plunged temporarily into beds of moist sand.*

Camellia

Primula
denticulata

Narcissi

Cultivated primrose

Helleborus niger

Polyanthus

Below: *Camellia flowers are so large and exotic you could easily believe they belonged to some tropical plant. In a cold conservatory, even the frailest flowered camellia varieties are seen at their best. Feed and water pot-grown camellias in late summer, two to three months before moving them under glass. Use a high-potash tomato feed to ensure that they produce a large number of flower buds.*

Growing begonias

Begonias belong to a large family of plants that includes both flowering and foliage varieties. The foliage types keep their leaves all year round, and include the striking metallic tints and strongly patterned leaves of *Begonia rex,* tall cane-stemmed begonias with oval, spotted leaves, and the many bushy species, often with distinctive bronze, plum or coppery foliage. These types do flower, but the flowers are much less conspicuous than the foliage. 'Foliage' begonias make superb specimen plants and look specially striking teamed with large brass or copper containers – an antique coal scuttle, for instance. Smaller plants are good for adding foliage effects to groups of brightly coloured flowering tropical plants. Of the flowering begonias, the best known are the tuberous types used for summer displays. The really large-flowered kinds are best grown under cover to protect the fragile flowers. To see these at their best, limit each tuber to a single stem by rubbing out all but the fattest growth bud when the plants first come into growth in spring, and remove the single female flowers later on. Use a large pot and a rich potting mix, feed heavily with liquid tomato feed and support the stem with a strong cane. During the winter, store the dormant tubers in a paper bag at room temperature. Other flowering begonias are also available; these do not grow from tubers and keep growing all year.

Left: Grow the pendulous varieties of tuberous begonias in hanging pots and jardinières, as their flowers nod downwards and are best seen from beneath.

Ideal conditions

Temperature: *16°C(61°F) min.*
Watering: *Keep mix just moist, never bone-dry or too wet.*
Feeding: *Quarter-strength liquid tomato feed. (For tuberous kinds, apply at normal strength.)*
Lighting: *Non-tuberous flowering begonias – good light, but not strong direct sun. Tuberous kinds – sun, but not strong midday sun. Foliage kinds – light shade.*
Winter care: *Tuberous kinds will be dormant. The others require little feed and reduced watering.*

Right: Keep winter-flowering begonias regularly fed, and remove the dead heads as the flowers go over. Cut back hard and repot when flowering finishes. Some types bloom almost all year.

Planting a corm

1 *To avoid planting the dry corm upside down by mistake, sit it convex side up in a dish of damp seed mix on a warm windowsill.*

3 *Press the base into a 10-13cm (4-5in) pot, leaving the tip just above the surface. Water; keep out of bright sun until growing well.*

Left: *The iron cross begonia (Begonia masoniana) is so called due to the dark pattern in the centre of each heavily textured leaf. The plants are just as easy to grow as* Begonia rex *and enjoy similar conditions, but they are prone to powdery mildew.*

Growth buds start to develop after two to four weeks.

2 When fat pink buds are visible, you can be certain it is the right way up, although no roots have appeared yet. Pot up the corm.

4 For the most spectacular results, remove the pair of small single female flowers on either side of the huge double male flower.

Above: *In this greenhouse, a superb collection of giant-flowered exhibition-quality begonias grows in the shade created by a thriving crop of melons. Both like a warm, humid atmosphere.*

Foliage begonia species occur in a huge range of leaf patterns.

Begonias are shade-tolerant and easy to grow.

Jungle-style pot covers add a designer touch to a small collection of foliage begonias.

Right: *Foliage begonias look good grouped together in unusual baskets. Line the containers with black plastic or stand the plants in saucers to stop water spoiling the wickerwork.*

Growing orchids

Orchids can become an all-consuming hobby, and many enthusiasts will set up a whole greenhouse or conservatory just to grow these plants. However, without buying specialist equipment, it is quite possible to grow some of the easier orchids, together with a collection of other plants that need similar conditions. If you can maintain room temperature (about 21°C/70°F) all year round, grow phalaenopsis and miltonia orchids with tropical houseplants, such as anthurium, maranta, philodendron, fittonia, etc., which all enjoy warm, humid light shade. Both these orchids continue growing all year round, and will flower again periodically when the new growth reaches the right stage of maturity. In summer, the temperature should not rise above 29°C(84°F). Garden centres often sell quite a good range of orchids but the best selection can be found at specialist orchid nurseries. Here the growers are real experts and will advise on the best type to grow in your conditions. They can also provide the best kind of feed, and also the special potting mix needed for repotting orchids. Do not use normal potting mix.

Above: Orchids like plenty of fresh air, and in a specially set up orchid house grow best on slatted staging, so that air currents can move up between them. Space plants out well to permit good air circulation around them.

Left: If you only grow a few, stand orchids on a tray filled with gravel or expanded clay pellets. Top up the tray with water so that humid air rises round the plants but they are not standing in water.

Right: A huge range of orchid types make good conservatory and greenhouse plants in the right growing conditions. Stand plants on upturned pots at the back of the staging to bank up the display and make them easier to see. Do not be tempted to overcrowd the plants.

Feeding orchids

1 Orchids only need very weak feeds. Use special orchid fertiliser at the recommended rate and do not overfeed the plants.

2 Water the diluted feed over the entire surface of the mix. Water drains quickly through orchid mix; pour away any excess.

Watering

Right: *Mist plants daily to keep the air humid. To avoid chalky spots from hard water, or chlorine damaging the foliage, use clean rainwater, or tap water that has been filtered, boiled and cooled, which removes chalk and chemicals.*

Water when mix looks dry. Avoid overwatering at the roots and do not leave plants standing in water.

Different potting mixtures

Finnish peat with foam rubber pieces and polystyrene to aid swift drainage when watering.

An inorganic mix of loosely packed rockwool and polystyrene granules. You supply all nutrients.

A young plant potted in good-quality fine bark can be repotted every six months.

Orchids root quickly into bark mix. It decomposes slowly, releasing most of the nutrients required.

Above: *Alternatively, plunge the pot into a basin for a few minutes, keeping the water level just below the crown of the plant to avoid soaking new growth and to prevent any loss of potting mix.*

Right: *This elegant Odontioda hybrid is one of many orchids that will thrive as a houseplant in a cool room. It can produce these lovely arching flower sprays at almost any time of year.*

Displaying orchids

In a greenhouse where the winter temperature is kept at 10°C(50°F), cymbidiums are the most suitable orchids. Miniature kinds take up much less room than the full-sized forms, which can grow 90-120cm(3-4ft) high and the same across. All cymbidiums need a resting period in summer. Wait until four to six weeks after the last frost, then stand them outdoors in a cool shady spot under trees. Protect them from slugs and snails during this time and do not forget to feed and water them occasionally, as they will not grow properly if allowed to become bone dry. Water them lightly until you bring them back under cover towards the end of summer, well before the first risk of frost. Do not stand other orchid species outdoors. They each have their own fairly precise requirements, so always follow the growing instructions on the label or advice provided by the nursery. It is not practical to treat them all the same.

Below: A few orchids in pretty pot covers give a conservatory an exotic tropical touch that teams nicely with rattan furniture. Glass-topped tables and a vinyl floor are a good idea as you can easily wipe up water spills.

Right: Fleshy white roots indicate an active root system on this cymbidium. The plump pseudobulbs (here cut in half for demonstration) of this species hold water reserves. Orchids such as phalaenopsis that do not have pseuodo-bulbs should never be allowed to dry out totally as they lack this internal reservoir.

A display with phalaenopsis

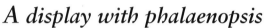

1 *Choose a phalaenopsis in bud or with flowers just opening, lift it out of its pot and remove the loose potting mix from the roots. (Do not use a plant growing in pure rockwool.)*

2 *Repot it into a clear glass tank filled with glass marbles and pebbles of different sizes. In the wild, orchids grow with roots exposed to light, so this will not harm the plant.*

3 Lean the plant across the tank and support it with a few large pebbles. Use more marbles to separate the stones. Aim for a display that looks good inside the tank as well.

4 With the plant in place, top up the tank with marbles to the rim then water very lightly, moving the can around as you do so. Do not add more than 1.25cm(0.5in) of water.

Keep the air around the plants humid by mist spraying.

5 Stand the tank on a table or shelf out of direct sun. Water evaporates up through the marbles and keeps the roots moist without causing them to rot.

A living basket of orchids

1 Place expanded clay granules into a plastic-lined basket. The moistened granules create a humid microclimate around the plants.

2 Arrange a foliage plant and some orchids outside the basket, then stand them in their final position. Leave them in their pots.

Ficus benjamina

Odontocidium 'Rupella'

Rossioglossum williamsonii

Masdevallia urosalpinx

Odontocidium 'Tiger Hambühren'

3 Hide the tops of the pots under a thin layer of small spreading ferns or moss; these also help provide extra humidity. Mist regularly with tepid water and stand out of direct sunlight.

Pieces removed when shaping the plant can be rooted as cuttings.

Indoor bonsai

True bonsai are outdoor plants that are not suitable for growing in a greenhouse or conservatory. However, some conservatory plants are very well suited to training and trimming and can be dwarfed by growing them in shallow dishes to create 'indoor bonsai' plants. Good plants to choose include dwarf pomegranate (*Punica granatum nana*), olive (*Olea europaea*) and *Cuphea hyssopifolia*, although you can often find small plants sold as 'indoor bonsai starter plants' in nurseries. Some of the plants sold as 'tots' for bottle gardens are suitable, especially those with small leaves. You can sometimes buy larger, ready-trained 'indoor bonsai' plants, often decoratively planted in shallow dishes, as well as partly trained plants in small bonsai pots, that look the part straight away. These only need occasional trimming to keep them to roughly the original shape, allowing for future growth. However, training your own plants from the start is fun, creative and much less expensive. The aim of 'proper' bonsai is to create a plant that looks gnarled and aged. You can follow regular bonsai techniques, using copper wires twisted around stems to pull plants into angular shapes if you wish. However, 'indoor bonsai' is much less serious; here it is quite permissible simply to exaggerate the plant's natural shape. Feel free to use 'props', such as granite chippings, small pebbles, craggy rock or driftwood to add an oriental note to a trimmed plant in a dish. Alternatively, prune a scrambling plant, such as *Ficus pumila*, to pick out the shape of a knotty dried plant stem. Indoor bonsai plants need frequent watering; being in such tiny containers, they dry out quickly. Apply a weak feed occasionally to avoid over-vigorous growth.

1 Cuphea hyssopifolia *grows into a bushy plant with 'tiered' branches. By snipping out the centre, you can create a plant with a wagonwheel-like shape when seen from the top.*

2 *Cleanly trim away all the bottom shoots, flush with the bark, to leave the lower 7.5-10cm(3-4in) of the plant with clean, bare stems.*

3 *Using bonsai scissors, slightly trim back the tips of the shoots so that they are all the same length and the plant becomes a neat umbrella shape.*

4 *Tip the plant gently out of its pot and tease apart the roots. Remove as much surplus potting mix as you can, but do not tear off too many of the small fibrous roots.*

5 *Use an old fork or a bonsai 'rake' to 'comb' the roots out gently. This removes a lot more potting mix without harming the fragile roots the plant needs to survive.*

6 *An old toothbrush dipped in tepid water makes a good bonsai-sized brush to clean up the plants' stems. Scrub gently to remove moss, algae and dirt, then rinse in clean water.*

7 Cut a square of the special plastic bonsai mesh used to stop worms getting into the pots, and place it over the drainage hole in the base. This also stops potting mix washing out.

8 Cut 10cm(4in) of flexible copper bonsai wire, make a hook at one end and thread it through the mesh over the drainage hole, leaving the wire poking up through the top.

9 Place a little bonsai potting mix in the bottom of the container. Spread out the plant's roots well and sit it to one side, angled slightly forward for an asymmetrical look.

10 Use the copper wire fixed to the mesh in the base of the container to keep the stem at the right angle. Bend it round the base of the stem to hold the plant in position.

11 With the plant firmly fixed, use a small spoon to scoop more bonsai potting mix around the roots. Cover all exposed roots to keep them from drying out.

Right: *The wiry stems and compact growth of* Serissa foetida *from Southeast Asia make it specially suitable for indoor bonsai. It is usually treated as a foliage plant but older specimens may produce small pink flowers. Keep it at above 7°C(45°F) in winter.*

Below: *Indoor bonsai make striking shapes that need clear space around them and an uncluttered background to be properly appreciated. For a striking display, use tiered staging at different heights. Do not be tempted to overcrowd the plants.*

Left: *The small-leaved species of ficus make good, easily grown bonsai and take well to training into various shapes. This* Ficus retusa *has been grown as a fairly natural-shaped bush. The small-leaved form of* Ficus benjamina *called 'Natasha' produces a similar-looking plant.*

Rattan units are ideal for cacti and succulents, which like dry air and do not need a lot of water splashed round them. The cane marks if it is kept too moist.

Below: *Cacti and succulents have naturally architectural shapes that look specially stunning when they are attractively displayed. Avoid overcrowding them, so that each shape stands out against the background.*

Cacti & succulents

Cacti and succulent plants are the perfect choice for a hot sunny conservatory or greenhouse. They need plenty of sun to remain in character and can tolerate lack of watering, high summer temperatures and occasional neglect better than any other plants. An enormous range of plant shapes and sizes are available from specialist nurseries, and many will flower regularly, even from an early age. If excessive sun and heat are a problem, choose the true cacti, which have waxy skins and spines, or 'wool'. Where growing conditions are hot and sunny but the temperature can be kept below 30°C(86°F) by shading and ventilation, a wider range of choice cacti and succulents will be happy. Many desert species of euphorbia make striking 'living sculptures' that look outstanding as large individual specimen plants grown in terracotta pots. Echeverias make neat rosette shapes with brightly coloured bodies in shades of pearly blue, grey, mauve and purple; a group of different kinds in a bowl looks sensational. For reliable flowering cacti, choose mammillaria, rebutia, notocactus and echinopsis. Group them in bowls with trailing succulents, woolly species, such as *Espostoa lanata*, and small prickly pear types, such as *Opuntia microdasys*, for contrasting plant shapes and textures. In a bigger area, a few large, striking specimen plants will make much more impact than many small plants, but a mixture of large specimens and bowls of attractively arranged smaller plants is the ideal combination for a good display.

Right: *A large collection of cacti looks attractive planted out into natural-looking, landscaped beds. Make these raised, so the plants are easier to see, and use a gritty, well-drained mix.*

Creating a cactus display

1 For a varied display, plant a tall, upright cactus towards the edge of a terracotta bowl filled with special cactus mix. Add a prickly pear and a small, globular flowering cactus.

2 Put in more cacti, separating plants of similar shape with contrasting kinds. Pieces of gnarled driftwood are good as decoration, or use pebbles or chunks of quartz.

3 Tuck more plants between the driftwood. Folded paper is useful for planting species that otherwise snag your fingers and sleeves.

Plant closely for immediate impact but give the cacti more space after a year or two.

4 Top up the cactus mixture with fine gravel. The easiest and safest way to work the gravel between the plants is to pour it slowly and carefully from a fold of paper as shown here.

Living stones

Living stones are unusual desert plants that mimic pebbles to avoid being eaten in the wild. Being tiny, you can cultivate a good collection in very little space. The species shown here are lithops, which have a short growing season in midsummer and flower in late summer. For the rest of the year the plants need to be left unwatered, when they concertina down to dry skins. Watering during the dry season can be fatal.

Below: Plant a group of lithops in a shallow bowl with gritty mix, and cover the surface with granite chippings. Add real smooth pebbles.

Cleistocactus jujuensis

Rebutia spinosissima

Opuntia microdasys rufida

Mammillaria bocasana

Mammillaria polythene

Parodia leninghausii

Mammillaria plumosa

Notocactus ottonis

Mammillaria elongata 'Cristata'

5 The finished bowl is ideal for a sunny spot indoors, but could stand outside in summer. An occasional shower keeps the plants clean.

Tender & exotic bulbs

Indoor bulbs add seasonal variety to a plant collection, and go very well with plain green, coloured and variegated foliage plants. Different species are available that between them flower virtually the whole year round. Garden centres stock a limited range of tender bulbs, but for the greatest choice buy from mail order bulb specialists. Since bulbs can only be sold through the post when they are dormant, summer- and autumn-flowering bulbs are sold in spring, while winter- and spring-flowering kinds are sold in autumn. They should all be planted as soon as possible after delivery. Many kinds have individual growing requirements, but as a general rule plant tender bulbs in pots of rich, soil-based potting mixture. Water in, then keep on the dry side until new growth is visible. Gradually increase the watering as growth speeds up, and begin liquid feeding with a high-potash liquid tomato feed about three months after planting. After flowering, continue to feed and water to build up the bulb for the following season's flowering. As the foliage starts to yellow, slowly reduce feeding and watering until the bulbs are fully dormant. Store them in their pots and keep the potting mixture virtually dry until shortly before the start of the following growing season. Then repot into fresh mixture, and a bigger pot if needed, and begin very light watering as before. Although most tender bulbs spend part of their year dormant as dry bulbs, some, such as clivia, eucharis and *Haemanthus albiflos*, are evergreen and keep their strap-shaped foliage all year round. Protect them from scorching sun or excessive drying out, as damaged foliage may take several years to 'grow out'. However, evergreen bulbs do need a little 'rest'; give them less water and a slightly lower temperature in winter. Repot or topdress with fresh potting mixture in spring.

Left: Lachenalia *flowers in early spring and spends summer dry and dormant. A sunny plantroom kept at 5-7°C(40-45°F) in winter is ideal for it. This is* Lachenalia aloides tricolor.

Growing hippeastrum

1 *Use a pot about 2.5cm(1in) wider than the bulb and add potting mixture so that the bulb will be half to one third exposed. Choose a healthy, undamaged bulb.*

2 *Hold the bulb upright and fill in with potting mixture, leaving a gap between the surface and the pot rim for watering. Water lightly and place in a warm, bright place.*

Right: Water sparingly until growing vigorously. Flowers appear on bare stems after about two months; leaves do not develop until later. Feed and water well in summer, and dry off gradually when leaves start to yellow.

Planting sprekelia bulbs

1 In spring, plant new bulbs or offsets and repot older plants. Leave the neck above the surface. Young bulbs and recent offsets are unlikely to flower in their first year.

2 Water lightly until leaves are growing vigorously. Feed regularly with tomato feed during the summer to build up the size of the bulbs, and they should flower the following year.

Right: Sprekelia formosissima *is very nearly hardy; keep it frost-free in winter. The deep red 'orchid' flower appears in summer. Keep the bulbs dry when dormant in winter; repot into fresh soil in spring.*

Allow foliage to dry off gradually in autumn.

Above: *Plant calla lily rhizomes in early spring. To avoid rotting, water lightly until plants are growing well. Then give more water and feed. Dry off gradually after flowering.*

Right: Haemanthus albiflos *flowers in autumn or winter. This evergreen keeps its broad leaves all year, so never let it dry out badly. It slowly forms large clumps; repot in spring.*

Right: Clivia miniata *looks good even when not in flower. Keep plants shaded and well fed and watered in summer. In winter keep them cool (7°C/45°F) and short of water, otherwise they will not flower.*

Growing spring bulbs

Pots of spring bulbs provide valuable seasonal decoration in a conservatory or greenhouse. Narcissi and hyacinths, just coming into flower, are sold in nurseries from midwinter onwards, ideal for putting into pretty pot covers or tucking into bowls of moss to make instant displays. The flowers last much longer in unheated or frost-free conditions than they would if taken indoors and used as houseplants; at room temperature the blooms go over very fast. Although buying ready-grown spring bulbs promises quick results, it is not difficult to grow your own, and far more satisfying. However, you need to know the 'tricks of the trade' to produce plants as good as those you buy. The process starts in autumn, when the first dormant bulbs appear on sale in nurseries. Buy early to be sure of getting the best bulbs; for growing in pots you need the largest bulbs, since these will have the most flowers. Select bulbs that are undamaged, do not show signs of mildew or blue mould, and have not started to sprout. For early flowers, choose tazetta narcissi (varieties include 'Paper White' and 'Grand Soleil d'Or') and specially prepared hyacinth bulbs. Plant tazetta narcissi in containers of potting mixture or bulb fibre with the tips showing, or for a more decorative result, plant them in clear glass bowls filled with smooth pebbles or glass marbles and water. Keep the bulbs at a temperature of 10°C(50°F) and top up the containers occasionally to keep the water level about 1.25cm(0.5in) below the base of the bulbs. They should flower about 12 weeks after planting.

Right: *Try growing narcissi in square glass flower vases. This way, the roots become part of the display. Expanded clay granules or grit in the bottom provide drainage. Use normal potting mixture. Take care not to overwater.*

Left: *In this unheated greenhouse, shallow terracotta pans of spring bulbs have been sunk to their rims in a bed of sand. This not only makes a good seasonal display, but also insulates the roots and keeps them uniformly moist, since the pots are porous.*

Right: *Small individual pots of daffodils make a great display; stand them in a basket and hide the tops of the pots with a layer of moss; this also helps keeps the roots cool and moist.*

Hyacinth bulbs

Hyacinth bulbs are available from late summer onwards. If wanted in flower for Christmas, choose specially prepared bulbs and plant them as soon as available. Plant unprepared bulbs in mid- to late autumn. Grow both in the same way. Plant into pots and stand pots outside in a cool, shady place. Water occasionally and protect from pests. Do not bring the pots inside until the plants produce flower buds just showing colour, or the flowers will not open.

1 Hyacinths grow well in pots. Grow them singly so you can pick plants at the same stage later on to make into a display. Half-fill 9cm(3.5in) pots with potting mix.

2 Gently press a bulb into the middle of each pot, then fill the pot to the rim with more mix. You should just be able to see the tip of the bulb. Tap lightly to firm.

3 Moisten the mix evenly, and allow surplus water to drain away. Stand the pots in a cool, shady place where the bulbs slowly form roots before foliage appears.

Right: To get bowls of hyacinths where every bloom is at the same stage of development, cheat. Choose identical plants growing in pots, and plant or plunge them into their final containers. Do not disturb the roots. Hide the pots with moss.

Above: Large buckets of spring bulbs make a good seasonal display under glass; the cooler the conditions, the longer the flowers will last. Keep them well away from heaters.

Below: Grow pots of the earliest spring bulbs, forced hyacinths and early daffodils in a cold greenhouse. Move them to the conservatory in bright pots for a welcoming display.

Growing gesneriads

1 Achimenes are sold as tiny scaly rhizomes during early spring. To make a good show, plant five to their own depth in a wide half pot.

2 Water and keep in a humid place at 13°C(55°F) or more until shoots appear. Move to a lightly shaded spot. 'Stop' leggy shoots to make a bushier plant.

Gesneriads are a very popular family of plants that includes streptocarpus, gloxinia (Sinningia speciosa) and achimenes (hot water plants). Although each has a distinct character, they all have large colourful flowers and all need very similar growing conditions. Treat them like African violets (the best-known gesneriad of all) and you will not go far wrong. Streptocarpus are evergreen plants that flower continuously all summer; in winter they like a cool rest at about 10-13°C(50-55°F), with a little less water than usual. In time, they form large clumps, but after a couple of years the plants start to show their age and are best replaced by young ones, which have a neater rosette shape and fresher-looking foliage, and flower more freely. New plants are very easily grown from leaf cuttings struck in late summer. Gloxinias have huge, velvety, bell-shaped flowers on plants that form a loose rosette of large, luxuriant, oval leaves. They grow from tubers, which are cultivated in the same way as begonia tubers, except that gloxinias are not suitable for growing outdoors. Keep them under glass and out of sunlight. At the end of the summer, the plants start to die down naturally and should be allowed to dry out gradually over the following six to eight weeks. Once the foliage has died, store the dry tubers in a paper bag in a cool dry room indoors, ready to start up again the following spring. Achimenes grow from strange scaly rhizomes, which are planted in spring just under the surface of the potting mixture. Like gloxinia, they need plenty of warmth to start them into growth, but do not be misled by the common name into thinking that they need watering with hot water. Tepid water is ideal. Achimenes make bushy plants, ideal for pots; some varieties have a trailing habit, well suited to indoor hanging baskets. The plants flower from mid- to late summer. When flowering finishes, allow the plants to dry off slowly until the foliage dries out. Cut this off just above the top of the pot and store the dormant rhizomes, still in their pots of dry potting mixture, in the same conditions as described for gloxinia tubers.

Right: Achimenes flower from mid- to late summer. The stems start to die down in autumn. Reduce watering until the mix is quite dry, and repot the new crop of rhizomes the following spring.

Gloxinia tubers

Before potting, sit tubers concave side up on a dish of moist peat until growth buds appear. This ensures that the tuber is the right way up.

1 Press the tuber into the centre of a pot almost filled with mix. The underside must make firm contact so that it starts rooting.

Ideal conditions

Gesneriads enjoy good light but need shading from direct sun, and like to be kept moist during the growing season. They grow best in a potting mixture containing plenty of peat or fibre; an equal mixture of peat-based and soil-based potting mixture suits them best.

Left: Episcia has very pretty decorative foliage and tiny flowers, which are usually red as in the case of this variety, E. 'Harlequin'. The naturally lax habit makes it ideal for hanging containers.

Right: Streptocarpus flowers all summer and into early autumn. In winter, it is semi-dormant but retains its leaves, so do not let it dry out. Maintain a minimum temperature of 7-10°C(45-50°F).

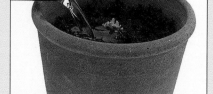

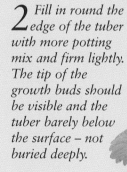

2 Fill in round the edge of the tuber with more potting mix and firm lightly. The tip of the growth buds should be visible and the tuber barely below the surface – not buried deeply.

3 Water lightly. The aim is to moisten the mix and consolidate it slightly around the tuber. Water lightly whenever the mixture looks dry until the plant is growing strongly.

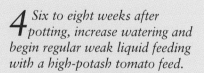

4 Six to eight weeks after potting, increase watering and begin regular weak liquid feeding with a high-potash tomato feed.

Below: The foliage forms a flattish rosette over the pot, with a cluster of large colourful bell flowers in the centre; plants keep flowering till late summer. Remove the dead heads.

53

Growing fuchsias

Fuchsias are enormously popular greenhouse plants. They are easy to grow and flower continuously throughout the summer and early autumn. Different varieties of fuchsia have either bushy, upright or trailing habits; look on the label or check catalogue descriptions to see which are which. Naturally bushy types make the best pot plants, upright types are the easiest to train as standards and trailing varieties are excellent for hanging baskets. Most fuchsias can be grown outdoors in summer, but those with particularly large flowers, such as 'Texas Longhorn' and the new 'Californian Dreamer' series, are much better grown permanently under glass as their large blooms soon deteriorate when exposed to the weather. The 'Californian Dreamer' series also need warm conditions to flower well. As well as the popular hybrid fuchsias, the species are becoming better known. These look quite different from the hybrids. The triphyllas are the best known, with long tubular flowers on rather upright plants. Other species include small, low, bushy or trailing plants with tiny flowers, such as *Fuchsia procumbens*, which produces edible fruit. *F. fulgens* makes a very large exotic-looking plant, with big leaves and bunches of long, dangling colourful flowers. *Fuchsia boliviana* is best grown as a climber, as its stems are tall and weak, but the flowers are superb. Cultivate species the same way as normal fuchsias, but give them much larger pots and more feed and water. Large species need some support.

Left: Fuchsia arborescens *is one of the species, and has large clusters of delicately scented flowers. It can make a good bushy pot plant if pinched back as a cutting.*

Propagating fuchsias from cuttings

1 *Choose the tip of a healthy, strong shoot and, using a sharp knife, slice cleanly through the stem about 10cm(4in) from the top, cutting just above a leaf joint.*

2 *Hold the cutting by the leaf, rather than the stem. Touching the stem can damage the fragile tissues of the young plant and cause problems with rotting later on.*

3 *Dip the base of each cutting into rooting hormone, if you wish, and then push each one to about half its length into an individual small pot or cell in a multiple seed tray.*

Above: Fuchsias are available in a huge range of varieties, having upright, bushy or trailing stems, large or small blooms, and big, flamboyant double or long slim tubular shapes. They are very collectable!

4 When the container is full, water in the cuttings and cover them with a transparent lid. This propagator-style lid is good, as it is equipped with two adjustable air holes for ventilation.

5 Pot fuchsia cuttings soon after they root. If left too long, they grow leggy and the roots become tangled so that they are damaged when you try to separate them. Use small individual pots and any good potting mixture.

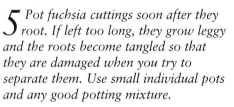

6 If you did not remove the growing tip of the cutting when it was taken, do so when it is potted. This ensures that the young plant grows bushy and does not get leggy.

Above: 'Mary' is a spectacular triphylla hybrid whose long tubular scarlet flowers contrast nicely with the long-oval, dark purplish-tinged foliage. It is quite an old variety.

Above: Fuchsia procumbens *is a New Zealand species with low, spreading, compact stems and strange flowers that are followed by edible fruit. More of a curiosity than a great beauty.*

'Space Shuttle', a hybrid of a species fuchsia, has very unusual flowers in striking colours. Like most species, the cuttings need stopping several times to develop a bushy habit.

Fuchsia fulgens rubra grandiflora *has flowers up to 10cm(4in) long. It will make a fine large plant and thrives in a spacious container.*

Growing pelargoniums

Pelargoniums enjoy heat and sun, and are fairly tolerant of neglect; they withstand occasional lapses in watering and ventilating, and recover quite well if allowed to wilt. They flower all the better for a rather tough growing regime; in fact, the commonest causes of problems are over-generosity with feed and water, which encourages over-lush leafy growth and soft stems with a tendency to rot at the base. There are several kinds of pelargoniums. The best known are the zonals, which have roughly kidney shaped leaves, often marked with a prominent dark band. Though seed-raised strains of these are used outdoors as bedding plants, choice, old-fashioned named varieties are much sought after by collectors. These are best grown under cover, as they need more careful cultivation and have larger flowers that are easily damaged by bad weather. Regal pelargoniums have showier – almost orchidlike – flowers and light green leaves. Miniature pelargoniums are specially collectable, making neat compact plants. Both zonal and regal types are available as miniatures, and all are glasshouse plants. Scented-leaved pelargoniums do not look like conventional pelargoniums and are grown for their scent; the flowers are often quite insignificant. This group can be grown outdoors in summer, but their perfumed foliage makes them good greenhouse and conservatory plants.

Left: Miniature regal pelargoniums such as this 'Sancho Panza', take up much less room. Deadhead regularly and 'stop' young plants once or twice to make them neat and bushy.

Taking cuttings from a pelargonium

1 *Remove the lower leaves with a sharp knife. To avoid cutting yourself, make sure the blade is not in line with your thumb.*

2 *Remove any developing buds and flowers. Now the cutting will have two or three leaves at the top and a length of clean stem.*

3 *Make a clean cut across the base just below a leaf joint. This is where the new roots will emerge. Ragged tissue left here would rot.*

Avoid overcrowding the cuttings in the pot.

4 *Dip the base of each cutting in rooting powder. Space cuttings around the edge of a 10cm(4in) pot. Water and keep moist until rooted.*

Above: *Regal pelargoniums are the aristocrats of the family with large, orchid-like flowers. They come in a wide range of bright colours. Shade them from the very brightest sun. They flower constantly from late spring until early autumn. Propagate from cuttings taken in late summer.*

Right: *Pelargonium graveolens is one of the scented-leaved pelargoniums, grown mainly for the citrus fragrance that is released when a leaf is gently crushed. The pale pink flowers are fairly insignificant. Old plants get leggy in time; take cuttings to replace them periodically.*

Below: *Regal and zonal pelargoniums grow to about the same size, in contrast to miniature pelargoniums (left). The miniatures are becoming very collectable.*

Ideal conditions

Despite their tolerance of heat and occasional neglect, pelargoniums repay correct cultivation. Neglected plants often develop tall, lanky, woody stems and lose their lower leaves. Pot the plants in a soil-based potting mix with up to 10% added sharp sand or potting grit to improve drainage. Feed occasionally with high-potash tomato feed in summer, and let the soil just about dry out between waterings. In winter they need a rest. Keep plants at a temperature of 5-10°C (40-50°F), stop feeding them, and leave plants longer between waterings. Replace old plants every year or two with young ones raised from cuttings struck in late summer.

Trailing plants

Some of the most difficult plants to accommodate indoors are those with a weeping habit, such as aeschynanthus, *Hoya bella* and *Ficus pumila* (creeping fig). However, they can look superb under glass, where there is plenty of bright, airy and otherwise empty roof space. A 'false ceiling' of flowers and foliage in attractive hanging containers provides light shade, or use groups of dangling containers on walls as the finishing touch that continues a ground level display up beyond eye level. Choose plants that suit the growing conditions and match your other displays, but select roof plants with special care, as conditions here are usually hotter and brighter than close to ground level. Trailing succulents, such as *Sedum sieboldii*, *S. morganianum*, *Ceropegia woodii* and *Senecio rowleyanus*, have a very contemporary look, with bizarre shapes. Tradescantia and chlorophytum are common foliage plants that are rarely seen at their best due to lack of suitable display facilities, yet take on a whole new look when grouped together in good hanging containers under glass. They are specially striking hanging in front of a mirror, which gives them added sparkle. Trailing plants also look good tumbling down in tiers from a multi-storey shelf unit; this is a good way to display small pots of compact, floppy plants, such as trailing fuchsias, episcia, and achimenes, rather than true trailers that need a long 'drop'. Turn plants grown on shelves round weekly – a quarter turn is enough – to prevent them growing one-sided.

Or allow them to grow one-sided deliberately for a flowering waterfall effect. Watering can be difficult where trailing plants live high up in the roof, but various gadgets intended for watering outdoor hanging baskets, such as long-reach hose attachments, are handy.

Left: This variegated form of Hoya carnosa *needs a free-draining cactus mix and some sun. It will climb or trail. Protect furniture from the sticky 'honeydew' that drips from the open flowers.*

1 *A rack intended for kitchen utensils makes a good 'chandelier' for displaying naturally lax plants, such as Beloperone guttata, especially where space is short.*

2 *Hang a short, colourful plant in a small basket at an angle for an informal look. This Aeschynanthus 'Hot Flash' is a new strain; compact and bushy but with a droopy habit.*

3 *You can also use longer trailing foliage plants to help vary the levels within the display. This one looks like ivy but is actually an easy-to-grow semi-succulent plant, Senecio macroglossus.*

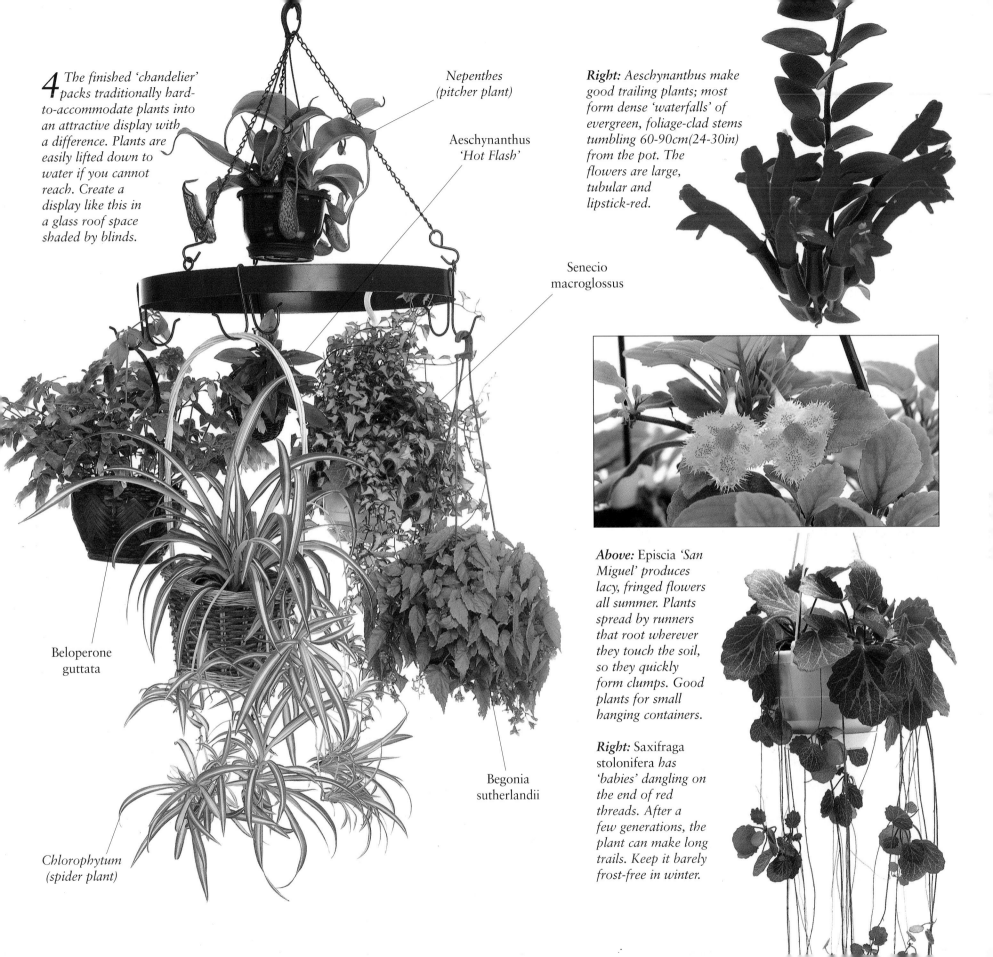

4 *The finished 'chandelier' packs traditionally hard-to-accommodate plants into an attractive display with a difference. Plants are easily lifted down to water if you cannot reach. Create a display like this in a glass roof space shaded by blinds.*

Nepenthes
(pitcher plant)

Aeschynanthus
'Hot Flash'

Senecio
macroglossus

Beloperone
guttata

Begonia
sutherlandii

*Chlorophytum
(spider plant)*

Right: *Aeschynanthus make good trailing plants; most form dense 'waterfalls' of evergreen, foliage-clad stems tumbling 60-90cm(24-30in) from the pot. The flowers are large, tubular and lipstick-red.*

Above: Episcia 'San Miguel' *produces lacy, fringed flowers all summer. Plants spread by runners that root wherever they touch the soil, so they quickly form clumps. Good plants for small hanging containers.*

Right: Saxifraga stolonifera *has 'babies' dangling on the end of red threads. After a few generations, the plant can make long trails. Keep it barely frost-free in winter.*

Connoisseur plants

A conservatory or ornamental greenhouse is ideal for growing plants that are too big to be houseplants but too tender to grow outside. Unusual 'conversation piece' plants also form a vital ingredient in the potential planting scheme. A plant that always attracts attention is *Medinilla magnifica*. This substantial tropical shrub has large oval leaves, and carries flowers like pink bunches of grapes all summer. It will grow in a very large container, but is best given a sizeable root-run in a soil border or raised bed and allowed to develop freely. It needs a tropical environment with high humidity, light shade and constant warmth all year round, and looks good grown with exotic tropical foliage plants. Another eye-catcher is *Impatiens niamniamensis* 'Congo Cockatoo', with its large red-and-yellow, beak-shaped flowers. This unusual impatiens species grows upright, with a thick succulent stem, and flowers all summer. For scent, the old-fashioned tea roses do best grown under cover. Climbing varieties, such as 'Maréchal Niel', do best in rich soil in a good-sized border against a sunny wall. Train and prune it in the same way as outdoor climbing roses. Bush varieties, such as 'Anna Olivier' (pale yellow) and 'Catherine Mermet' (lilac-pink), are generally compact and suitable for growing in 38cm(15in) pots filled with rich, soil-based potting mix. Water generously in summer and feed regularly with a liquid rose feed, or use a good brand of liquid tomato feed that contains magnesium and trace elements, as well as a high-potash formulation. Find unusual plants at nurseries specialising in conservatory plants.

Above: Medinilla magnifica *makes a large, striking, specimen shrub. Give it warm humid conditions, shade from strong sun, and a minimum winter temperature of 16°C(61°F).*

Left: Here, the striking shape of Pachira aquatica *has been accentuated by plaiting three seedlings together. Keep it humid and well watered, and at room temperature in winter.*

Right: The bottle-shaped main stem of Jatropha podagrica *loses its leaves in winter. This succulent requires little water in summer and none in winter, when it should be kept at a minimum of 10°C(50°F). The sap is irritant.*

Below: All the leaves and flowers of the unusual Impatiens niamniamensis *are clustered near the top. Old plants look leggy, so take cuttings and start new plants each spring or summer.*

Left: Anigozanthus produces clumps of evergreen leaves and bunches of long, narrow, tubular flowers. Water well in summer, much less in winter, and keep it frost-free then.

Above: Grevillea lanigera 'Mount Tamboritha' *is a compact form with a low sprawling shape, ideal for a raised container or the foreground of a group. The curly flowers are fascinating.*

Below: Basella rubra *is a fast-growing plant with weak stems that need support. The large mauve-tinged leaves make a good background for the clusters of pink flowers.*

Below: Cestrum violaceum *(was* Iochroma violacea*) has large clusters of long, tubular, smoky purple flowers throughout summer and autumn. This medium-sized bushy shrub grows vigorously in summer and rests in winter.*

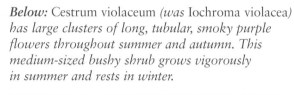

Left: Old fashioned tea roses make superb conservatory shrubs for large pots. They need frost protection in winter. This is Rosa 'Maréchal Niel' *which is very fragrant and disease-resistant.*

61

Growing bromeliads

Bromeliads are a striking family of evergreen plants shaped like stars, rosettes or sometimes upright 'urns', which hold water in a hollow reservoir in the centre. Some species, such as dyckia, are semi-succulent and like plenty of sun, but most of the best-known kinds, including cryptanthus and tillandsia, enjoy light, humid, shady conditions. They like plenty of fresh air and a temperature between 10-30°C(50-86°F) that fluctuates quite a bit between night and day. Some species grow in soil, such as aechmea and neoregelia, but some can be wired to cork bark and hung up on a wall; this is a dramatic way to display a collection. Alternatively, tuck moss into a tube formed from small mesh wire netting and push the plants into it, or make a bromeliad 'wall' of mesh stuffed with sphagnum or hung with Spanish moss – itself a species of tillandsia. Bromeliads are grown mainly for their fascinating body shapes, patterns and colours. However when they reach full size they will flower; some – *Tillandsia cyanea*, *Billbergia nutans* and *Aechmea fasciata* – have spectacular flowers.

Above: Vriesia 'Charlotte' makes a neat pineapple top-shaped plant with a broad spreading spike of flowers; the geometric shape suits a plain, smart pot cover.

Below: Guzmania are dual-purpose plants that can either be grown in pots of soil or wired to cork or driftwood and grown epiphytically in high humidity. This cultivar is 'Claret'.

Potting up an offset

Aechmea chantinii

Daughter

Mother

1 After flowering, it is normal for a bromeliad plant to die, but first it usually produces one or more offsets. Wait until these are a good size and the mother is going over.

2 Knock the plants gently out of their pot and lever the offset, plus as much of its root system as possible, away from the old plant; the parent plant will be discarded.

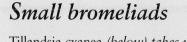

Small bromeliads

Tillandsia cyanea (below) takes up little room and flowers reliably every year. Grow it in a pot or wired to cork bark or driftwood.

Above: Cryptanthus bivittatus, *commonly known as earthstars, are small, starfish-shaped plants with stripy arms. Though happy in shade, in full sun they take on pink or red tints.*

Above: *The blushing bromeliad, Neoregelia tricolor 'Perfecta', lets you know when it is going to flower because the centre of its leafy rosette turns red. A few other bromeliads do this, too.*

3 Clean up the offset by removing any dead baby leaves from the base. Check to see if there are any pests, such as scale insect or mealy bug, which often hide in the crevices.

4 Pot the offset into a container only slightly larger than its roots; bromeliads have a small root system. Use a free-draining potting mix or add 10% grit to a standard mixture.

5 Fill the hollow central vase with water. Top it up regularly all year if the plant is in a warm place. Water the mix lightly, then keep it barely moist; bromeliads do not like wet feet.

6 Provide light shade and humid air. Offsets grow faster if left with their mother as long as possible. If plants form several offsets, pot them all on and let them grow into a big clump.

Airplants

Airplants are a popular group of bromeliads with a unique way of life: they are able to grow without any roots. In the wild, it is true, they use their rudimentary roots for clinging onto tree bark and rocks, but everything that a normal plant does with its roots, such as taking in water and nutrients, airplants do through their leaves. As house and conservatory plants, this gives them tremendous creative potential as they need not be grown in pots; they are much happier clinging on to something. Airplants can be lodged in crevices in gnarled chunks of tropical driftwood, cork bark or porous tufa rock, glued to chunks of mineral ore, or arranged in ornaments. They can even be suspended from threads to make mobiles. Since individual plants are quite small, an attractively grouped collection makes a much better display. Their fantastic shapes lend themselves to contemporary or abstract arrangements, but they can also be teamed with tropical plants that like similar conditions, such as maranta, fittonia and ferns, for a more naturalistic display. Airplants need constantly high humidity, bright indirect light but no strong sun and a temperature of 10-30°C(50-86°F) to thrive.

1 Choose an attractively gnarled chunk of wood (cleaned tropical 'driftwood' is sold in florists' shops). Wedge the base of the largest plant firmly in place into a natural crevice.

2 Sit airplants with a wide base such as this into depressions in the log. They look more natural when placed at a slight angle, rather than completely upright.

3 Continue adding more plants; smaller or relatively leafless species often look better when grouped in twos or threes. It also adds more variety to the overall display.

4 If necessary, glue the plant in place with airplant glue. Put a blob of glue on both the base of the plant and the wood, press and hold the two together until set.

5 Use tiny plants at the front to create foreground detail; this is especially important in a display such as this where plants are too stiff to spill out over the edges.

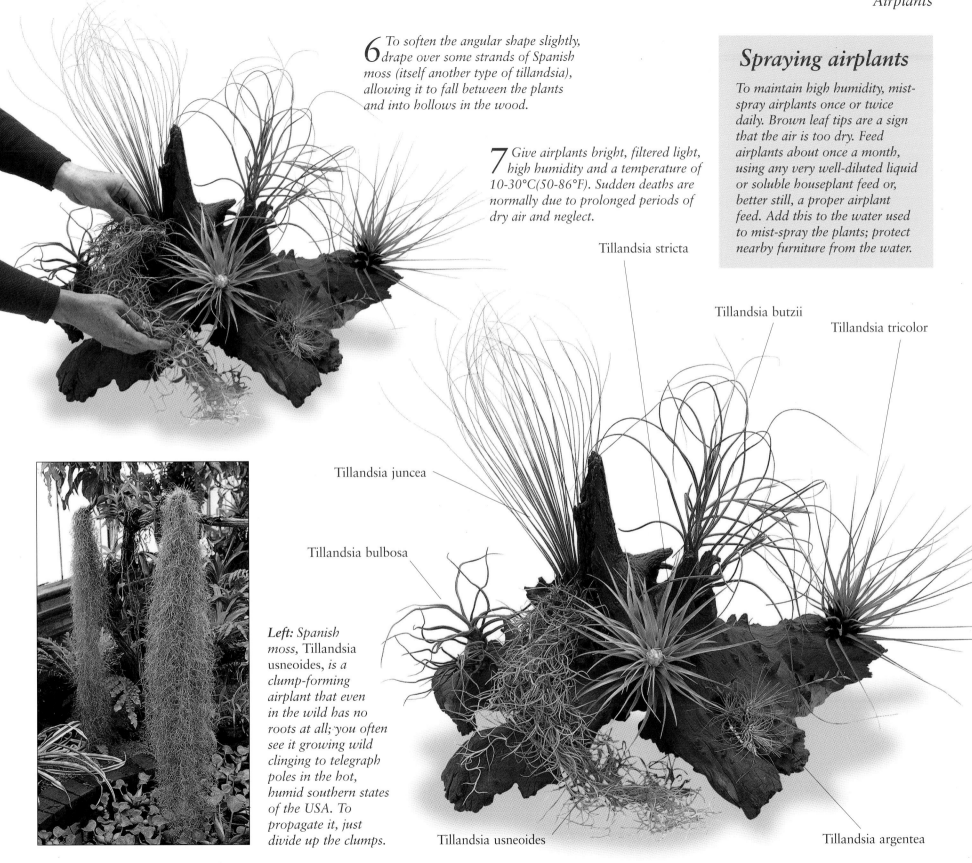

6 To soften the angular shape slightly, drape over some strands of Spanish moss (itself another type of tillandsia), allowing it to fall between the plants and into hollows in the wood.

7 Give airplants bright, filtered light, high humidity and a temperature of 10-30°C(50-86°F). Sudden deaths are normally due to prolonged periods of dry air and neglect.

Spraying airplants

To maintain high humidity, mist-spray airplants once or twice daily. Brown leaf tips are a sign that the air is too dry. Feed airplants about once a month, using any very well-diluted liquid or soluble houseplant feed or, better still, a proper airplant feed. Add this to the water used to mist-spray the plants; protect nearby furniture from the water.

Tillandsia stricta

Tillandsia butzii

Tillandsia tricolor

Tillandsia juncea

Tillandsia bulbosa

Left: *Spanish moss,* Tillandsia usneoides, *is a clump-forming airplant that even in the wild has no roots at all; you often see it growing wild clinging to telegraph poles in the hot, humid southern states of the USA. To propagate it, just divide up the clumps.*

Tillandsia usneoides

Tillandsia argentea

65

African violets

African violets (saintpaulia) are amongst the most popular collectors' plants. They are available in a good range of colours, with double, semi-double and single flowers. Miniatures and variegated foliage forms are also available from specialist nurseries, which regularly bring out new named varieties. The greatest range of plants is usually available from these nurseries or at their stands at flower shows. Although mainly thought of as houseplants, African violets are also ideal for a conservatory that is shaded from bright sun, where the temperature can be controlled at a reasonably steady 21-27°C(70-80°F), with high humidity in summer. In winter they need room temperature (16-21°C/61-70°F). Remove the shading then so that they receive brighter light, which is vital if the plants are to flower all year round. African violets team well with tropical houseplants and orchids, which enjoy similar growing conditions and make a good display together. African violets also grow very well under artificial lights, and this is the ideal way to cultivate them in a very shady conservatory or one with a solid roof that does not get much direct light. Or you can use artificial light to supplement natural daylight in winter and keep the plants flowering.

Left: Picotee varieties of African violet have prettily 'edged' flowers in various colours.

Rejuvenating an old African violet

1 Old African violets often look a bit unsightly as they lose their lower leaves and form clumps that spoil their good 'dinner plate' shape, with flowers grouped in the centre.

Pot up the offset as below

2 In spring, knock an old plant out of its pot and carefully separate any offsets. Slightly tease apart the ball of roots with your fingers to avoid damage to either plant.

Potting up the offset

1 Deal with the offset first. Remove any damaged or broken leaves and those with very long leaf stalks that spoil the shape, leaving a neat rosette for repotting.

2 Choose a new pot only slightly bigger than the root system. Sit the rosette in the middle and fill the gaps with fresh potting mixture. Tap it lightly down to consolidate.

3 Taking the old plant, remove all dead or damaged leaves around the base, leaving a clean stem. Tease out part of the rootball close to the base to remove some old potting mix.

Growing under lights

The best way to accommodate a large collection of plants is on shelves with fluorescent tubes above them; consult specialist firms for advice. On a smaller scale, you can buy 'plant lights', which resemble normal light bulbs, but produce natural daylight instead of yellowish light. They fit into table or desk lamps and can be used to 'spotlight' plants attractively, at the same time as providing good growing conditions. Position artificial lights quite close to the plant – about 30cm(12in) away – so that the light intensity is strong enough, and leave the lights on for 12 to 16 hours each day. To ensure that lights are turned on and off regularly, plug them into a timer switch. When watering plants, take care to avoid wetting electrical fittings; in a conservatory, plug into a current breaker for safety.

Right: To ensure that flowers are bunched in the centre of the plant, always separate offsets so that you only have one plant in each pot.

Below: Group several African violets in plain, matching pot covers to make an attractive mini-display with a range of different coloured flowers.

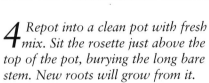

4 Repot into a clean pot with fresh mix. Sit the rosette just above the top of the pot, burying the long bare stem. New roots will grow from it.

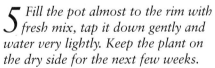

5 Fill the pot almost to the rim with fresh mix, tap it down gently and water very lightly. Keep the plant on the dry side for the next few weeks.

6 Both plants will soon develop the characteristic posy shape, with a frill of foliage encircling a spray of flowers. Do not feed for four to six weeks, since the new mix contains enough nutrients.

Bougainvillea

Bougainvilleas flower all summer and make an exceptionally good subject for conservatories and greenhouses. They enjoy heat, dry air and bright light and thrive in extreme conditions that equal neglect for many other conservatory plants. Due to their increasing popularity, specialist nurseries now stock a huge range of named varieties in all flower colours as well as the traditional purple: pink, yellow, red, lavender and amber, and with variegated foliage. When grown outdoors, bougainvilleas are capable of covering a villa wall in a couple of seasons, but they need not take up so much room. In a conservatory they certainly make a superb flowering feature trained out over trellis, but they can also be confined in a reasonably sized pot and trained into space-saving shapes, such as standards, or over topiary frames to form flowering pillars or pyramids. A few varieties are naturally compact and make superb subjects for hanging baskets. Choose a variety such as 'Raspberry Ice', which is not only compact, but also strongly variegated and makes a particularly good show when used in this way. Simply secure the stems around the sides of the basket to make a stunning 'nest-shaped' plant, ideal for hanging in a greenhouse or conservatory roof in full sun. Bougainvilleas are easy plants to grow. They need a very free-draining potting mixture, so make up your own using any good-quality soil-based mix and add about 10% small bark chippings. Use this to fill individual containers or a raised bed for a wall-trained plant.

Above: Bougainvillea grows well in strong sun and heat close to the glass. When trained over the inside of the conservatory roof, it creates light dappled shade, which other indoor plants enjoy.

Above: The bracts of the compact variety 'Mahara Pink' start off brownish-pink. As they mature, the colour gradually changes to a pale pink.

Ideal conditions

Bougainvilleas enjoy plenty of sun and tolerate heat and dry air, but grow and flower best when fed and watered regularly in summer. Tie the fast-growing stems to supports to keep the plants tidy, but beware of spines, as they are quite prickly. In winter, keep the potting mix much drier and the temperature below 10°C(50°F); this 'rest' is essential or the plants will not flower the following year. Prune lightly after flowering, and in early spring shorten the previous year's stems back close to the main framework of the plant to prevent it getting too big. Grow in a free-draining mix; the one used for citrus plants is ideal.

Propagating bougainvillea

1 Take a non-flowering, semi-ripe shoot with about seven leaves in summer. Remove the lower leaves. Cut off the base below a leaf joint.

2 Cut any remaining large leaves in half to reduce water loss and increase the chances of survival. A humid atmosphere helps rooting too.

3 Dip the base of each cutting in water, then into rooting powder. Push each cutting into an individual peat pot.

The roots grow through the sides of the peat pot so you can pot them on without damage.

Left: 'Raspberry Ice' is specially attractive due to its variegated foliage and bright flowers. Its very compact growth makes it ideal for small containers or hanging baskets.

Bougainvillea 'Elizabeth' is of medium vigour, ideal for wall training.

B. 'Rainbow Gold' has orange-brown bracts with cream centres.

Above: B. 'Elizabeth' has strong magenta-coloured bracts that contrast well with the deep green leaves.

Nip out tips in late winter to keep in shape.

Left: In a hanging basket, spread out the stems of a compact variety such as this 'Alexander' to cover the base and supports. Tie in the growing stems.

Standard plants

Plants that normally grow big and bushy, such as clianthus, datura and bougainvillea, can all be trained as standards so that they take up less room. Large fruiting plants, including citrus, figs and even grape vines, can also be trained in this way. Then shade-tolerant plants can be grown underneath the plants, right up to the trunk, which not only lets you grow more plants, but also makes a much better display. However, it is not only exotics that are worth training into 'ball-headed trees'. Many quite ordinary plants, such as pelargoniums, lantana and abutilon, show themselves in a totally new light when trained as standards. Regal pelargoniums and large-flowered species fuchsias, such as *F. boliviana* and *F. arborescens*, look especially showy. But virtually any woody plant can be trained into a lollipop shape, as long as its natural habit is bushy and not sprawling or trailing, so why not be adventurous and experiment with any of your favourite plants? Whatever you grow, the technique is basically the same as for training standard fuchsias. Begin forming a standard plant in spring, as close to the start of the growing season as possible, as this gives you the rest of the summer to see some results.

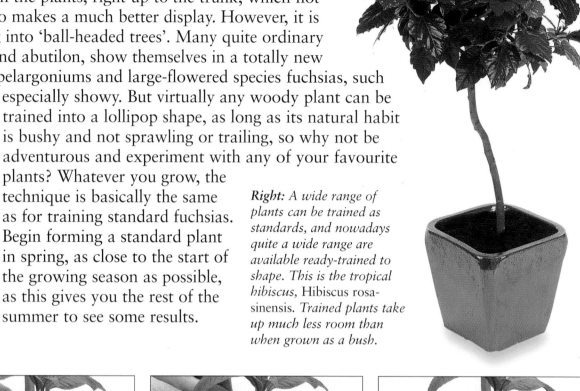

Right: *A wide range of plants can be trained as standards, and nowadays quite a wide range are available ready-trained to shape. This is the tropical hibiscus, Hibiscus rosa-sinensis. Trained plants take up much less room than when grown as a bush.*

Creating a fuchsia standard

Move the plant to a pot one size larger and filled with fresh mix. Push in a cane next to the stem.

1 *Select a rooted cutting with a strong, straight, unbranched stem. Bush varieties of fuchsia have a naturally upright habit that makes them easier to train as standards than trailing varieties, which have weak, drooping stems.*

2 *To encourage the stem to grow straight right from the start, secure it to a cane every 15-20cm(6-8in). This plant tie is a metal ring that you just clip into place around the plant. There are other alternative plant ties.*

3 *Soft string takes longer to tie, but is less likely to mark the stem or trap leaves. Put the first tie just above the rim of the pot, and add another one to support the soft new growth at the top every few weeks as it grows.*

4 *A 'trainee' standard plant needs regular feeding and pest control to keep it growing well. Push in a slow-release feed stick and an insecticidal stick. These release feed and pesticide each time the plant is watered.*

Left: Left to grow naturally, olives eventually make very large trees. Training them as standards in pots makes them into ideal specimens for a conservatory that is kept frost-free in winter.

Right: Standard azaleas look much showier than their more common short bushy counterparts. Plants are rarely available and expensive to buy, but given time you can train your own.

5 Nip out sideshoots regularly, but not the leaves. When the main stem reaches the top of the cane, allow the top five sideshoots to develop before nipping out the growing tip.

6 As the plant matures, the main stem becomes a leafless, brown and woody trunk. Rub out any sideshoots while they are tiny. If allowed to develop, they spoil the shape of the plant and can kink the stem.

Other shapes

Once you have experience of standard plants, you might try more advanced shapes – domes pyramids or obelisks. Use the same techniques of supporting stems, removing unwanted shoots and 'stopping' the ones you want to develop into bushier growth. Topiary frames are a useful support and guide when training complicated shapes.

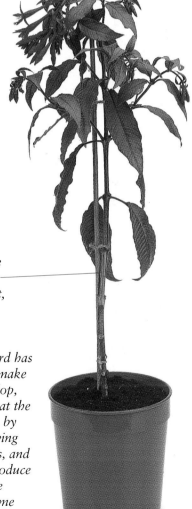

If you begin with a nursery plant, prune away all the stems except the straightest, most upright one.

7 The basic standard has been formed. To make the bushy head develop, 'stop' the sideshoots at the top of the main stem by nipping out the growing point after five leaves, and when they in turn produce sideshoots, repeat the process again each time they have five leaves.

Citrus plants

Citrus plants add a special ambience to a conservatory. Their clusters of pearly white flowers are heavily perfumed, and a single plant is enough to fill the room with fragrance. Unlike many plants with scented flowers, citrus plants continue blooming over a long period – even while they are carrying fruit – so their air-freshening effect can be maintained almost all year round, including in winter if plants are kept sufficiently warm. To get the best out of citrus plants, they need proper care. Just before the start of the growing season in spring, repot plants into a rich, soil-based potting mix, combined with 10-15% of bark chippings or 20% perlite. Begin watering more frequently as plants start to grow, but do not water little and often. Instead, wait until the mix is virtually dry, then water thoroughly and leave until the soil is almost dry before watering again. In winter, plants need watering much less often than in summer, especially if they are kept cool. Feed regularly in late spring and summer, when the plants are growing fastest. Use special citrus plant fertiliser or a high-nitrogen liquid feed. In summer, citrus plants can stand outdoors on a sheltered sunny patio. They can remain under cover as long as the temperature is kept below 30°C(86°F). In winter, citrus plants must be protected from frost. If the potting mixture is kept almost completely dry, most kinds tolerate temperatures just above freezing. (The most reliable kinds for cold winter conditions are Meyer's lemon and kumquat.) However, plants are more successful kept at 10°C(50°F) in winter, and at room temperature they will continue flowering and fruiting all year round.

Right: Kumquat is one of the hardier citruses, and tolerates a winter temperature of 5°C(40°F). The small fruit look decorative but taste sharp, and are usually sliced into summer drinks.

Ponderosa lemon

Meyer's lemon

Grapefruit

Thomson's navel orange

Seville orange 'Bouquet de Fleurs'

Left: A huge range of fascinating citrus fruit can be grown in the shelter of a warm conservatory (10°C/50°F) in winter; the flavour of fresh-picked fruit is quite different from that of shop-bought fruit.

'Garey's Eureka' lemon

Calamondin oranges

Oval kumquats

Limequats

Tahiti lime

Left: The variegated calamondin orange is a particularly good all-year-round conservatory plant due to its good foliage, strongly perfumed flowers and profusion of small fruit.

Right: Citrus limon 'Garey's Eureka' is a popular variety for commercial crops because of its heavy crops and long season.

Left: Left unchecked, citrus plants make untidy bushy shrubs, but they can be pruned as short standards with a single trunk. The top can be trimmed to form a tidy dome shape.

Above: The pink flower buds of 'Garey's Eureka' (formerly 'Four Seasons' lemon) are an attractive feature of the plant. They open into fragrant white flowers.

Left: Citrus aurantium 'Bouquet de Fleurs' is one of the bitter oranges, with very heavily scented flowers. The fruits are grown commercially for oil of neroli used in eau-de-cologne.

Planting mixture

Citrus plants need well-drained conditions at the roots. Make up a special potting mixture consisting of 80% soil-based potting mix combined with 20% perlite for drainage, and add slow-release fertiliser granules. (Follow the manufacturer's advice for the correct rate).

Soil-based mix

Perlite

Conservatory climbers

Vigorous climbers are the perfect way to make use of every available space under glass. Grow them on trellis against a wall or up over the roof, where they provide decorative summer shade without blinds. Plants that lose their leaves in winter make the best 'living shade', as they allow in more light when conditions are naturally dull. Greenhouse varieties of grapevine with their large foliage are very good for this purpose, and the developing bunches of grapes add interest. Choose muscat types for a heated house; these have the richest flavour and hang on the vine into the new year. Of the climbers with scented flowers, jasmines are outstanding; choose tender varieties, such as *Jasminum sambac* (Arabian jasmine) or *J. grandiflorum* 'De Grasse'; both have white, powerfully scented flowers. *Mandevilla suaveolens*, also called Chilean jasmine, has large, white, strongly scented, trumpet-shaped flowers. Unfortunately, climbers with more colourful flowers are rarely scented, so choose spectacular shapes and colours instead. *Chorizema ilicifolium* is smothered in clouds of small, airy, orange-and-purple flowers that look great against the tiny, holly-shaped leaves.

Hardenbergia and kennedia both have exotic pea flowers in various colours, But some of the most spectacular large climbers are passionflowers. The biggest – *Passiflora quadrangularis* – is a very fast grower; keeping it in a large pot helps to control its size. The flowers are almost 15cm(6in) across and dramatically patterned in bright red, purple and white. Many passifloras, including this one, produce both pretty flowers and well-flavoured fruit. The best fruiting species is *P. edulis*. However all passifloras need pollinating in order to set fruit, so it is vital that two flowers are open at the same time. Hand pollinate them with a soft brush.

Right: Mandevilla splendens *'Rosea' is a large woody Brazilian climber that can reach 6m(20ft) high with flowers up to 10cm(4in) across. Keep it compact by growing it in a pot and coiling the stems round supports.*

Left: Add to the jungly look of Mina lobata *by growing it in an ethnic pot cover and trailing the stems up a natural twiggy support. This one is made from dried garden prunings.*

Mina lobata

Mina lobata *(syn.* Ipomoea lobata*) is a vigorous climber. Though perennial, it flowers in its first year from seed, so treat it as an annual. The flowers all grow to one side of the spike, and change colour as they mature, from red buds to orange-yellow then cream. All three colours are open on the same flower spike at the same time, giving a fascinating three-tone effect.*

Above: Mina lobata *is very free-flowering and produces a good show of colour all summer long. Where there is enough room, train it up trellis, canes or on a wall.*

Right: *Passion-flowers have a constant succession of large, spectacular flowers throughout the summer. This striking Passiflora caeruleoracemosa is suitable for an unheated house as it can withstand light frost.*

Left: *Plumbago capensis is a floppy shrub, best trained against a wall to keep it tidy. Shorten the stems after flowering to tidy it, and then in early spring prune it harder so it stays compact and bushy.*

Above: *Grape vines trained out over the inside of a conservatory roof create light dappled shade underneath and help keep the room cool without using blinds or shading paint – but keep bugs under control.*

Right: *One of the most colourful scramblers for a cold or frost-free conservatory is Chorizema ilicifolium. Grow it in ericaceous mix combined with 10% grit for good drainage and prune it after flowering.*

Conservatory shrubs

Conservatory shrubs are ideal for a heated house with space to stand large pots on the floor. The very best plants are those that make a good shape and have interesting – often evergreen – foliage, as well as seasonal flowers. *Tibouchina urvilleana* fits the specification neatly; the large oval leaves have a soft furry texture and the purple-blue flowers appear over a long season. Oleander is another favourite (although all parts of the plant are poisonous); bottlebrush has large, exotic, red bristly blooms. Another popular choice is plumbago, which has intense sky-blue flowers all summer. Its weak stems are best trained out flat over a wall or against a support framework. Brugmansia (datura) have long, trumpet-shaped flowers in various colours and make large plants; the foliage smells rather unpleasant so stand them where they will not be touched. Most popular conservatory shrubs are available in garden centres, and can often be bought inexpensively as small 'starter' plants ready for potting on, but more unusual species are available from specialist nurseries.

Correa, for example, are a group of bushy, Australian, winter-flowering shrubs with small leaves and masses of bell-like flowers in shades of pink and green. Tender shrubby salvias have spectacular flowers, quite unlike those of the better-known bedding plants, and make substantial bushy plants with large spikes of red or blue flowers. Most conservatory shrubs can be cut back after flowering to keep plants tidy and within an acceptable size. Most are happy with a winter temperature of 7-10°C(45-50°F).

Left: Sutherlandia frutescens *has bright red flowers in spring and early summer, followed by inflated seedpods that turn bronze when mature. Overwintered at 8°C(46°F), these evergreen plants can live for several years.*

Left: Solanum rantonnetii *has blue potato flowers all summer. Left to grow naturally, the weak stems produce a sprawling shrub, but it makes a fine standard and also looks good trained against a wall.*

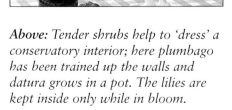

Above: *Tender shrubs help to 'dress' a conservatory interior; here plumbago has been trained up the walls and datura grows in a pot. The lilies are kept inside only while in bloom.*

2 *If the plant is very potbound, tease a few of the biggest roots gently away from the mass. Sit the plant in the middle of the pot.*

3 *Add more mix, keeping the plant at the same level as before. Firm in and water. Drain and wait till mix begins to dry before watering again.*

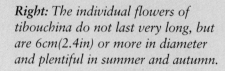

4 *Nip out the growing point at the very tips of each main shoot. This encourages new shoots lower down the stems and makes the plant bushier.*

Right: The individual flowers of tibouchina do not last very long, but are 6cm(2.4in) or more in diameter and plentiful in summer and autumn.

Below: Metrosideros 'Thomasii' has bottlebrush-like flowers set against grey-green leaves. Pinch out shoot tips or prune plants lightly after flowering. Keep at 4°C/39°F (minimum) in winter.

Below: Lantana has spectacular globe-shaped heads of flowers that change colour as they mature. Plants are very prone to whitefly; standing them outside in summer helps if you do not like to spray.

Left: Brunfelsia has large single blue flowers that only last three days and change colour every day, hence its common name: yesterday, today and tomorrow. It makes a large shrub that needs room to develop.

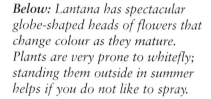

Right: Grevillea lanigera *has extraordinary bunches of curved flowers; this variety is 'Mount Tamboritha'. Unlike many grevilleas, this one is relatively small, with lax stems that make it a good plant for a hanging basket.*

Conservatory trees

One or two larger plants can make a conservatory look instantly 'landscaped'. They are a good way of decorating an area with plenty of furniture, where it is impractical to house large displays of small plants. Many conservatory trees can be stood outside during the summer, allowing a winter plant room to be turned into a summer sun lounge. In fact, many nearly hardy species prefer to be outside in summer; the cooler conditions mean that plants need less watering and are less susceptible to pests and diseases than under glass. However, in a permanent display, indoor trees have an important role to play by providing a contrast in scale. A single specimen tree makes an eye-catching feature standing on its own, or a good focal point in a collection of potted conservatory shrubs. Many suitable plants, both flowering and foliage kinds, are available. Of the flowering types, acacias are specially popular for their early spring flowers, often heavily perfumed, and they also have good foliage that makes a useful feature for the rest of the year. Together with *Albizia julibrissin* 'Rosea', the silk tree, and the coral tree, *Erythrina crista-galli*, it is nearly hardy. Frangipani adds a tropical look, but it needs room temperature throughout the winter. For foliage, some of the best conservatory trees are evergreens, such as *Cupressus cashmeriana*, *Pinus montezumae*, a tender pine with very long dangling needles, and tender eucalyptus.

Below: Frangipani (Plumeria rubra) *is a tropical tree with thick succulent stems and few leaves. The flowers are waxy and heavily perfumed. Keep it above 12°C(54°F) in winter, when it loses its leaves.*

Right: Cupressus cashmeriana *has blue 'sweeping' foliage and looks most spectacular when allowed to develop into a large specimen. Keep it compact by growing it in a smallish pot.*

Above: Albizia julibrissin *has mimosa-like foliage and large pink flowers with lots of silky threadlike petals. It is almost hardy and likes to be stood outdoors on the patio in summer.*

Seeds and stones

You can also grow fascinating and unusual non-hardy trees, such as tropical spices, from seed, and date palms, avocados or lychee trees from fruit stones. However, although they make interesting foliage plants, they are unlikely to flower or fruit in a conservatory. Plant stones and pips fresh from the fruit.

Left: *A group of conservatory trees makes a good background to smaller plants, and could stand alone as living sculpture to decorate a conservatory used as an 'outdoor' dining or living room.*

Left: *The coral tree,* Erythrina crista-galli, *is a prickly, fast-growing tree that produces its stunning flower spikes while still a young plant. Prune after flowering to keep it compact. In winter, keep it dry and frost-free.*

Right: Acacia armata *is naturally fairly compact and flowers while small, unlike many 'mimosas', which make large trees that need plenty of space to flower. However, it does have rather prickly stems.*

79

Scented plants

A conservatory or warm greenhouse is the perfect place to grow scented plants, as their perfume is most pronounced in warm, still, humid air under cover. Some plants are night-scented and best grown in a conservatory used as a sitting or dining room where they will be most easily appreciated. If growing plants especially for perfume, choose those with scented leaves or a long flowering season, as they give best value. Some scented flowers are only out for a short time, but do not ignore them as they contribute a delightful seasonal ambience to the conservatory display. Of the smaller flowering plants, heliotrope are the most indispensable. They flower all summer with a perfume like cherry pie. Old-fashioned named varieties, such as 'Chatsworth' are the best for scent. Many modern hybrids raised from seed are entirely without perfume. Frost-tender lavenders, such as *Lavandula dentata* and *multifida,* are wonderfully fragrant. The pineapple sage *(Salvia rutilans)* has strongly pineapple-scented foliage and pretty spikes of tubular red flowers produced throughout the summer. Gardenia is one of the most exotic perfumed plants, but can be tricky to grow. Some relatively unusual conservatory shrubs are worth hunting out for their scented flowers. Several frost-tender species of buddleja, such as *asiatica* and *officinalis, Camellia sasanqua* cultivars, *Genista fragrans* and *Clerodendrum fragrans* are all good. For night scent, choose *Datura inoxia* or *Cestrum nocturnum.* In an unheated house, *Rosmarinus lavandulaceus* makes a good semi-prostrate plant for a hanging basket. The foliage is strongly scented of balsam. To accentuate the scent of aromatic plants, feed them regularly but avoid overwatering, as this 'dilutes' the concentration of natural oils in the plant.

Below: *Scented-leaved pelargoniums need similar growing conditions to the zonal and regal pelargoniums, but unlike them the scented-leaved kinds have small, uninteresting flowers.*

'Atomic Snowflake'. Lemon rose scent with large yellow-variegated leaves.

'Iden Rose'. Pretty but small single pink flowers and a strong rose scent.

'Royal Oak'. Mauve flowers and pungently scented, oak-shaped leaves.

'Creamy Nutmeg'. Nutmeg scent, with small cream-edged leaves.

'Lady Plymouth'. Variegated lacy-looking foliage and a strong spicy rose scent.

Left: *Varieties of Camellia sasanqua need the protection of a conservatory in winter as they flower earlier than garden species. As their flowers are also strongly perfumed (unusual for camellias), this makes them doubly valuable for winter displays. In summer, stand them outside.*

Right: Datura inoxia *(syn Datura meteloides) has huge white or pale violet trumpet-shaped flowers that only last a day or two, but are freely produced throughout summer and autumn. During the day they are unperfumed; the strong heady fragrance is only released at night.*

Lilium longiflorum

Stephanotis

Gardenia

Left: *Some of the most strongly perfumed conservatory plants have white flowers, such as these longiflorum lilies, climbing stephanotis and the lime-hating gardenia. Grown together they can be a bit overpowering; 'dilute' the effect by blending them with other plants.*

Below: Heliotropium x hybridum *'Mrs. Lowther' is an old-fashioned variety of heliotrope whose flowers have the true cherry pie scent. Propagate it by cuttings in spring or late summer. Deadhead plants regularly to ensure continuous flowering throughout the summer.*

Foliage plants

A good collection of foliage plants forms the backbone of a year-round planting scheme. The shapes, textures and leaf colours act as a backdrop for seasonal flowers of all kinds, and even when nothing is in bloom, foliage plants make most attractive features of their own. Foliage plants are an investment; given good care they should keep growing and earning their keep for a great many years – often, indeed, until they outgrow the space available. A great many beautiful tropical foliage plants can be used in a house heated to room temperature, but in one that is kept unheated or frost-free in winter you need to be more careful with your choice of plants. Make the most of plants such as *Fatsia japonica* 'Variegata', cordyline palm, yucca and the various kinds of asparagus ferns. Unusual variegated plants, such as *Coronilla valentina glauca* 'Variegata', *Tulbaghia violacea* 'Silver Lace' and silver- or gold-variegated rosemary add fine detail; these and coloured-leaved coprosma species are worth hunting out. For something larger, pittosporum, especially varieties with dramatically silver- or gold-variegated evergreen leaves, are another good choice. Use striking feature plants, such as *Pseudopanax crassifolius*, which has tall, upright stems and long, narrow, saw-toothed, olive-and-cream mottled evergreen leaves, or *Arundo donax* 'Variegata'; its bold green-and-white leaves are strung along tall, upright, reedlike stems. Several species of sophora make fascinating, often craggy, shapes and have lacy-looking foliage. Another plant with natural character is the rice paper plant, *Tetrapanax papyrifer*, which has enormous mealy-backed greyish leaves. Several not quite hardy pines make stylish foliage plants for under cover; choose *Pinus patula* and *P. montezumae*, both with extravagantly long, drooping needles.

Above: Tolmiea menziesii *does well in a shady spot in a conservatory kept at about 5°C(40°F) in winter. Small plantlets grow from the tips of mature leaves, so an old plant trails slightly.*

Mini plants in a trug

To build up a good collection of houseplants, buy mini plants sold in tiny pots for bowl gardens. You can also arrange them temporarily, still in their pots. When they outgrow the display, pot them up and use them as normal pot plants.

1 *Line a wooden trug with thin plastic and add a thick layer of live moss, bark chippings or smooth pebbles.*

Left: Caladiums are grown for their striking tropical foliage. The plants grow from tubers and are completely dormant in winter. In the summer they need constant warmth and high humidity.

Left: *A conservatory need not be full of flowers to look impressive. A few stunning specimens, well displayed in striking pots, good backgrounds and unusual structures for climbers work well, too.*

Right: *For a real jungle effect, mix foliage plants with a wide range of leaf colours, textures and sizes. They provide a year-round backdrop to a display of seasonal flowering plants.*

2 *Choose a selection of mini plants that enjoy similar growing conditions; these foliage plants need light shade, warmth and humidity.*

Remove individual plants if they 'go over' or grow too big, and put another mini plant into the space. Or use a few flowers in a small jar.

Below: *The finished arrangement can stand on a shelf or table top. Keep the moss moist to maintain humidity around the plants, and water just enough so the roots do not dry out.*

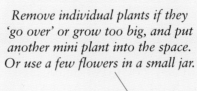

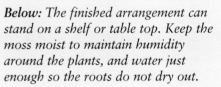

3 *Sink the pots into the moss, putting plants with contrasting leaf shapes and textures next to each other. Fill the trug well for instant impact.*

A pool feature

If you want a really striking and unusual centrepiece for a conservatory or decorative greenhouse, consider a water feature. This can be something as simple as a large glass or ceramic bowl of water on a table, containing a handful of floating plants – water hyacinth (*Eichhornia crassipes* 'Major'), water lettuce *(Pistia stratiotes)*, water chestnut *(Trapa natans)* and fairy moss *(Azolla caroliniana)* all look good grown this way. These warmth-loving plants need to overwinter in frost-free conditions and will grow happily in a conservatory all year round. For a more substantial feature, stand large, potted, tender water plants in a big container of water. Arum lily *(Zantedeschia aethiopica* 'Crowborough') and umbrella plant *(Cyperus involucratus/alternifolius)* or its giant cousin papyrus *(Cyperus papyrus)* all grow in water just covering the top of their pot, and look striking in a container that is wide enough to make the most of their dramatic reflections. Where small children make safety a priority, any of the wall fountains, pebble pools and similar water features that are used outdoors can be constructed inside a conservatory. The sound of running water and a humid atmosphere are perfect for a shady conservatory kept at room temperature all year round to house tropical plants.

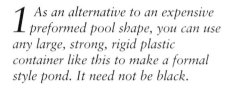

1 As an alternative to an expensive preformed pool shape, you can use any large, strong, rigid plastic container like this to make a formal style pond. It need not be black.

2 Buy or make enough log roll to encircle the container. It needs to be the same height as the container, so if necessary saw it to size first. Treat it with coloured wood preservative.

3 Place the container where you want the finished pond to stand, as it will be too heavy to move once it is filled with water. Position the log roll round it when the paint is dry.

4 Fill the container with water to within about 15cm(6in) of the rim. This allows room for displacement when you add the plants and pond pump without flooding your floor.

5 Place a clean flower pot upside down in the base of the container, close to one side. Check that it is the right height to raise your water plant to the correct level in the tub.

6 *Cyperus is a graceful indoor plant that enjoys standing in water. Sit it on top of the upturned flower pot. The top of the rootball should lie just below the water level when the tub is completely filled.*

7 *Sit a small, low-voltage submersible pump on the floor of the container. Add water to within 2.5cm(1in) of the rim.*

Right: Nymphaea 'Judge Hitchcock' is an ideal tropical water lily for the conservatory. The plants flower all summer, their colourful blooms slightly raised out of the water.

8 *Adjust the fountain head until it is flush with the water surface, and alter the flow rate so it produces a gentle gush of water. A tall fountain would splash and soon empty the container.*

Making a pool

Make a pool with a wide 'lip' all round and use it to display water-themed ornaments, such as china frogs or Indonesian wood carvings of tropical flowers. Surround the pool with large pots of tall conservatory shrubs to create an exotic jungly appearance. If you can keep the conservatory warm and humid all year round, include plants such as hibiscus, alocasia and maranta. Otherwise, choose plants such as citrus, datura and lantana, or those featured in the arrangement shown here, which only need to be kept a few degrees above freezing in winter to ensure a truly striking display.

Tibouchina urvilleana

Cyperus involucratus

Basella rubra

Cestrum violaceum *(syn.* Iochroma violacea)

Grevillea lanigera

Achimenes (hot water plant)

Bowl gardens

1 This is a bowl garden with a difference, made in an antique Victorian wash basin complete with its jug, which stands in the middle. Part-fill the basin with potting mix.

In a large space, small plants tend to look 'lost'. The solution is to group them together into imaginative arrangements. Arrange plants into large containers filled with potting mixture, or 'plunge' the pots to their rims in moss or bark chippings to make more temporary displays. Under cover, you can use wooden trugs, bamboo pot covers, or baskets made of wicker or exotic materials such as palm leaves. Line them with plastic first to protect them from damp potting mixture. If plants in pots are only to be plunged temporarily into moss or chippings, then a loose piece of plastic cut roughly to shape is all that is needed. If the container is to be filled with potting mixture, staple a well-fitting liner firmly inside the rim of the container. You can also use glass and ceramic kitchen dishes, antique fish kettles, china washbasins or similar containers, which are both attractive and practical. As they do not have drainage holes in the bottom, mix charcoal granules into the potting mix and take great care with watering. Very ornamental containers look best teamed with relatively plain plants; otherwise choose a container that picks out one colour from the leaves or flowers of the plants for a coordinated look. Tiny plants, such as the 'tots' or bottle garden plants sold in nurseries, look superb clustered closely together in this way. Arrange plants and 'props', such as chunks of quartz, slate shards, piles of glass marbles, etc., to make mini-landscapes in wide shallow bowls.

2 Choose a mixture of indoor plants, with foliage and flowers in a complementary colour scheme, and begin planting the basin. There is only room for one row of plants around the edge of the jug.

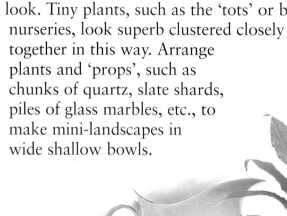

3 Plant the most striking plants at the front of the display and use filler plants around the back, where only occasional glimpses of foliage will be seen. Choose plants that all need similar growing conditions.

4 To balance the handle, plant a taller flowering plant on the opposite side of the bowl. It stops the display looking too symmetrical and gives it a more informal feeling.

Gynura sarmentosa *(velvet plant)*

7 *Water the plants in lightly, bearing in mind that there are no drainage holes for any excess to run away. It is easier to add more later than to deal with a swamp. Mist everything over.*

8 *The finished display looks good on an old-fashioned dresser or pine coffee table in a conservatory. This selection of plants needs good light but not direct sun, high humidity and a minimum temperature of 13°C(55°F) in winter.*

Tiny plants will need repotting into larger containers within a few months at most.

5 *When the basin is full, fill the jug to within 10cm(4in) of the rim with expanded clay pellets (as sold for greenhouse benches) as a clean, light-weight alternative to grit for drainage.*

6 *Choose a suitable plant as the centrepiece; this spreading begonia species is ideal. Sit the pot on top of the clay granules; the rim should be just level with the top of the jug.*

Begonia fuchsioides

Spathiphyllum wallisii *(peace lily)*

Justicia guttata *(shrimp plant)*

Pilea repens

Selaginella rubra *(club moss)*

Hypoestes sanguinolenta *(polkadot plant)*

Terrariums

1 *A glass case, such as an aquarium, makes a good-sized terrarium. Spread 2.5cm(1in) of well-washed gravel over the base for drainage.*

2 *Next add some potting mixture. Spread it out in a layer roughly 5cm(2in) deep, but do not mix it up with the gravel underneath.*

3 *Add horticultural charcoal (10-15% by volume) to prevent the potting mix going sour due to lack of drainage. Combine it with the mix.*

4 *Choose some craggy pieces of driftwood or, as here, dried ivy stems pulled down from a tree and cleaned, and place them in the tank.*

Some tropical plants, such as fittonia, maranta and selaginella, are tricky to grow because they have very thin leaves that are quickly affected by dry air, draughts and changing temperatures. Terrariums, bottle gardens and glass cases are the simplest way of growing them in a constantly still, humid atmosphere, and also provide a very decorative setting. In small bottle gardens and terrariums it is best to plant slow-growing species, such as the three listed above, since once the container becomes overcrowded it has to be completely dismantled and replanted. A larger glass case is easier to plant up and the wide open top makes it much simpler to add or remove plants. Greater depth means there is room for more 'landscaping'. You can include pieces of driftwood or gnarled stem and larger plants, such as climbers, as long as they have a support. If the top is left open, there will be enough air circulation for some flowering plants; the best are those that naturally enjoy high humidity and hang on to their flowers for a long time, such as African violets, or small orchids, such as phalaenopsis. Remove any dead flowers to avoid disease. Given a sufficiently large case, you could install heating cables in the base and artificial lights overhead, thus allowing you to grow exotic tropical plants in a conservatory that would normally be too cold or shady for them.

5 *Position the largest plant first – a climber. Rest the stems over the driftwood, then plant the roots into a pocket scooped in the potting mix, where they are hidden behind the climbing frame.*

6 *Unscramble the stems of the climbing plant and drape them along the branches of the climbing frame, so that they look as if they are growing naturally. Cut off a few stems if they look congested.*

7 Add a small, low, spreading plant – here Selaginella apoda – to balance the climber. It also disguises the rootball at the base of the climber.

8 Use a spatula or spoon to make a hole for planting the other plants, and use it to push back the potting mixture around them afterwards.

9 Add more plants, choosing those with a good range of leaf colours and textures, but avoid flowering plants, as their petals cause mildew.

10 A piece of cork bark makes a good background for a choice plant. Buy it from a florist or nursery. It will not decompose in damp soil.

Bottle gardens

A bottle garden is just a smaller and less elaborate version of a terrarium. Like a terrarium, a bottle garden provides an enclosed environment that is naturally draught-free and has high humidity, which makes it perfect for the fussier types of (usually tropical) houseplants. Being smaller, bottle gardens are most suitable for small, slow-growing, compact types. Many garden centres sell bottle garden plants, but check carefully before buying, as many sold this way are actually just small houseplants that will soon grow too big. Peperomia, selaginella and hypoestes are ideal.

Above: *An open-topped glass bowl makes an attractive container for one small, slow-growing bottle garden plant such as this maranta, which needs a humid atmosphere.*

Left: *There is no need to buy a special container to make a small bottle garden. Look in secondhand shops for an old sweet jar such as this or use a glass vase or kitchen bowl.*

11 Water lightly after planting, trickling water slowly down the inside of the glass to avoid soil splashes.

Epipremnum 'Neon'

Cordyline 'Red Edge'

Selaginella martensii

Hypoestes sanguinolenta

Selaginella apoda

Ficus pumila 'Sunny'

Didymochlaena truncatula

Index to plants

Page numbers in **bold** indicate major text references. Page numbers in *italics* indicate captions and annotations to photographs. Other text entries are shown in normal type.

Credits

The majority of the photographs featured in this book have been taken by Neil Sutherland and are © Quadrillion Publishing Ltd. The publishers wish to thank the following photographers for providing additional photographs, credited here by page number and position on the page, i.e. (B)Bottom, (T)Top, (C)Centre, (BL)Bottom left, etc.

Peter Beales Roses: 61(BL)
Eric Crichton: 26(TR), 46(BR), 50(BL), 51(BL), 65(BL), 68(TL), 79(TC), 81(BR)
Garden Matters: 49(CL, John Feltwell), 79(BL, John & Irene Palmer)
The Garden Picture Library: 15(BR), 27(TR, Brian Carter), 27(BR, Friedrich Strauss), 51(BR, Mayer/Le Scanff), 54(BC, Bob Challinor), 71(TR, Lamontagne), 72(TR, Friedrich Strauss), 73(BL, Mayer/Le Scanff), 83(TR, Brian Carter)
John Glover: 10, 12(T,B), 13(TR,BR), 14(BL), 28(TC), 34(TR), 50(TR), 75(L), 76(BR), 82(TR), 85(TR)
Harpur Garden Library: Cover (designer Maggie Gundry)
Sunniva Harte: 15(TR), 37(BR)
Andrew Lawson: 14(T), 35(BR), 83(TL)
S & O Mathews: Half-title page, Copyright page, 22(BL), 27(TL), 33(TC), 37(TR), 39(TR), 48(TR), 57(L), 75(CR)
Photos Horticultural Picture Library: 49(TR), 60(TR), 75(BR), 78(BL), 79(TL), 80(TR), 81(TR)
Plant Pictures World Wide, Daan Smit: 49(BC), 74(BR)
Geoffrey Rogers: 24(BR & inset), 27(BL), 45(TR,CR,BR, Paul Goff), 80(B), 81(BL)
Derek St. Romaine: 15(TL)

Acknowledgments

The publishers would like to thank the following people and organizations for their help during the preparation of this book:

Architectural Plants, Nuthurst, Horsham, West Sussex; Burnham Nurseries, Newton Abbott, Devon; Peter Beales Roses, Attleborough, Norfolk; The Citrus Centre, Pulborough, West Sussex; Floors 'N' Walls Ltd., Longfield, Kent; Holly Gate Cactus Nursery, Ashington, West Sussex; Hozelock Ltd., Haddenham, Buckinghamshire; Carol Gubler at Little Brook Nurseries, Ash Green, Hampshire; Hills Nurseries; Murrells Nursery, Pulborough, West Sussex; Gill and David Oakey; Graham and Susan Spears at Old Barn Nurseries, Horsham, West Sussex; Pots and Pithoi,Turners Hill, West Sussex; Read's Nursery, Loddon, Norfolk; The Tile Shed at Polhill Garden Centre, Sevenoaks, Kent; Wilma Rittershausen; Vesutor Air Plants, Billingshurst, West Sussex.